VOWS OF ❖ SILENCE

David,

Your an angel!

Thanks for getting me Jayne's number -

Love!
Diana 2012

DIANA LOUISE MICHAEL

VOWS OF SILENCE

A true story
of a survivor's triumph
over rape, teenage suicide,
and **religious abuse**

FOREWORD BY
STEVE ALLEN

Trust Publishing

Library of Congress Catalog Card Number: 93-60458

ISBN 0-9634910-4-0

Cover Design by Scott Andre

Printed in the United States of America.

First Edition: September 1993

This work is dedicated to God

for keeping the Light in me

through the darkness.

CONTENTS

Foreword by Steve Allen ix

Preface. xi

Acknowledgments. xiii

Introduction. xv

CHAPTER   1   *"Scarlet Ribbons"*. 1

CHAPTER   2   *"How Much Is That Doggie In The Window?"*. 5

CHAPTER   3   *"Mr. Sandman"*. 9

CHAPTER   4   *"I Say A Little Prayer"* 13

CHAPTER   5   *"You'll Never Get To Heaven"* 21

CHAPTER   6   *"Please, Mr. Postman"*. .31

CHAPTER   7   *"Michael, Row The Boat Ashore"*. 41

CHAPTER   8   *"Help"*. 53

CHAPTER   9   *"Soldier Boy"*. 59

CHAPTER 10   *"Light My Fire"*. 65

CHAPTER 11   *"Love Child"*. 73

CHAPTER 12   *"Where's The Playground, Susie?"*. 81

CHAPTER 13   *"Black Magic Woman"*. 91

CHAPTER 14   *"You've Got To Change Your Evil Ways"*. 97

CHAPTER 15   *"Chapel of Love"*. 107

CHAPTER 16   *"The Sounds of Silence"*. 119

CHAPTER 17   *"Don't Make Me Over"*. 127

CHAPTER 18   *"Hit The Road, Jack"*. 133

CHAPTER 19   *"Smoke Gets In Your Eyes"*. 139

CHAPTER 20   *"Mama Said There'd Be Days Like This"*. . . . 145

CHAPTER 21   *"I'm Still Standing"*. 153

CHAPTER 22   *"I Am A Rock"*. 159

CHAPTER 23   *"Killing Me Softly"*. 165

CHAPTER 24   *"Could I Have This Dance?"*. 173

EPILOGUE   *"Imagine"* 177

Illustrations following page 86

FOREWORD

If Diana Louise Michael were a purely fictional character, a professional editor would reject her story as inherently preposterous.

It occurs to most of us late in life, and to some of us probably not at all, that there would appear to be no justice whatever in the workings of the great natural universe. What precious little justice we do encounter is all imposed by humans. This is assuredly a sobering reflection, but since it conforms quite comfortably to the massive accumulation of sensory evidence, it must be faced, as must all truths.

But the great unfairness is even worse than that, for justice and good furtune are by no means apportioned evenly. Some are, from the very moment of their conception, granted numerous advantages. At the opposite end of the spectrum, however, there are those whose lives are characterized by a thousand-and-one painful slings and arrows.

And yet it is part of the great and no doubt eternal mystery of life that not all of those who are rich in advantage maintain their good fortune to the grave. There are also cases of those who begin the race of life far behind the starting line and yet somehow manage to improve their situation.

Such a person is Diana Louise Michael.

We know there is suffering in this world; we observe it every day and, because of the modern technology of communication, we are more aware of it than any previous generation. But we would still tend to doubt the reasonableness of Ms. Michael's story were it only the product of an author's imagination.

Her early life was unfortunate from the start. Diana's mother, a devout Catholic, suffered from uterine tumors after giving birth to three children, all boys, under the age of seven.

Despite medical advice to have no more children, Diana's mother became pregnant again and when she was due to deliver, her doctors, who could hear no fetal heartbeat, informed her that she would have a stillbirth. To their surprise she delivered premature twins, the second of which, named Diana, weighed only four pounds.

Life is difficult enough for premature children even at present. In the late 1940's many did not survive. Improperly administered radiation treatments further damaged the mother's system. As a result of which she became addicted to amphetamines and barbiturates.

It is difficult enough for even a normal healthy young woman to raise five children under the age of seven. For Diana's mother, giving such care was even more difficult.

Although religion brings comfort to many, Diana's mother had no such luck. She became a recluse, obsessed rather than comforted by her faith, and racked by excessive guilt—a guilt Diana did not understand until many years later when a shocking revelation provided the explanation.

Diana herself suffered from guilt on the groundless belief that she was personally responsible for her mother's suffering, believing her birth had caused it. As if the general chaos of her early years was not bad enough, she was, at age fourteen, the victim of an awful crime. Just as religion had failed her, so did the services of psychiatrists who misdiagnosed her case. After escaping from the hospital, she attempted suicide but *somehow* survived. It was at this point I first heard of Diana Louise Michael.

Having seen my television shows, she concluded—correctly as it turned out—that I might be sympathetic to her plight and wrote to me, confessing to her suicidal emotions. Something about the advice I was able to provide seemed to give Diana a reason for hope. Perhaps I should explain that many public figures receive a certain number of letters from deeply troubled people. It is not that difficult to write a letter of sound advice, but I have always been disappointed that it was not possible to do more for the various troubled souls with whom I have communicated over the years.

Separated as we were by so much space and time, I could have no direct effect on Diana's personal fate, which continued to be almost impossibly negative and destructive.

Diana, a relentless young woman indeed, has survived the remarkable blows that life has thrown at her. We can all learn from her story. All of us suffer disappointments, setbacks, even tragedies. Perhaps, from this young woman's history, we can learn something of the human capacity for survival and the ability of hope to bring us through even the darkest days.

Steve Allen

PREFACE

When I was eighteen years old, I took a "fatal" overdose. I have always known that I had a near-death experience and was asked to return to share the truth in *Vows of Silence*. Even though it took twenty-five years, I never gave up because I wanted to give people hope, the kind I needed when I was a suicidal teenager.

I recently retrieved that near-death experience under hypnosis. My soul left my body and was guided by spiritual beings to a conference room where many spirits were around a long conference table and telepathically communicated with me and tried to convince me to return to my body and complete my life on earth. These beings were loving and made no judgments about my suicide attempt.

"Please don't make me go back!" I begged, wanting to stay in their loving presence. There was suddenly a white sheet of paper on the conference table. When I focused on it, one word appeared on the paper in large block letters.....T R U T H.

The next thing I knew, two angels escorted me back to my body. I asked why I had to go back. They answered, "You will return, change your beliefs, transform your life, and show others how to do the same." They promised, "We will be with you from now on."

When I came out of hypnosis, I felt a deep love in my heart. It burned intensely like a flame in the center of my being. There is an incident in this book I describe where I was taken down a hospital corridor by two orderlies. I remember that I felt and saw two glowing angels on each side of me. At the time, I thought I was hallucinating, although I had felt this great love emanating from them. Now, I know they were my guardian angels keeping their promise. They have been with me, keeping me alive, through many life-threatening moments described in *Vows of Silence*.

Religious abuse is the misrepresentation of God, usually by traditional religion, not only the fringe cults people believe are so dangerous. It is very subtle abuse and, like verbal abuse, leaves no visible scars. When you think of God do you feel guilt, fear, shame, or hatred? Somewhere along the line you probably have been programmed to believe an untruth about God and this affected your self-esteem or the judgments you made about others.

As adults, we can permit ourselves to examine our given

religious beliefs to see if they are self-destructive and only choose to keep what is truly spiritual. Our soul knows what is the truth.

We would not think of wearing our parents' clothes, but without even a thought, we wear our parents' religion, often uncomfortably, knowing it does not fit our unbounded Spirit or the limitless forgiveness of God.

We have faced our dysfunctional families. Now it is time to face our dysfunctional religions.

ACKNOWLEDGMENTS

Many more people than I can thank on these pages have helped bring this book from thought to reality. I believe everyone I meet in life is my teacher.

I thank those who have loved me, and even those who invalidated me, for giving me the tenacity to move forward through many rejections to the publication of *Vows of Silence*.

TO MY FAMILY:

MOTHER, whose spirit supports me, for the perfect plot and setting in which to begin my life script.

FATHER, whose example, loyalty, intelligence, resilience, and love have given me stability and strength.

DONNA, my twin sister and "wombmate," for her unconditional love and for saving my life.

PETER AND TERRY, my brothers whose spiritual journey has enhanced my own, through their teacher Maharishi Mahesh, who brought Transcendental Meditation to the Midwest.

DAVID, my oldest brother, the hero of my childhood, who died of a heart attack at age 47, master guitarist, and the first seeker of the family.

KENNETH DEAN, my talented, handsome son. It was just the two of us for ten long years, "Tiger." You gave me a reason to live through those years of traumatic survival. I release you to God's care, your true Mother and Father.

BILL, my spouse and closet shaman. You have not abandoned me, even when my path has wandered far from yours. You are my earthly guardian and the light of the rest of my days on earth.

TO MY MENTORS:

STEVE ALLEN, who made me laugh! A man with the mind of a philosopher, the heart of a poet, and the soul of a wise man.

JUNE BECK, my counselor, my mother by transference. Thank you for healing my child and letting me leave home without a DSM III label!

EMILY CROFFORD, a great author and teacher, who taught me to hear my writing "voice" and to call myself "writer" because I write.

ECHO BODINE, psychic healer, my "nurserymate," whose classes in spiritual development changed my path forever.

GARY DALLEK, hypnotherapist. A gentle, spiritual man who helped me remember who I was, who I am, and who I am becoming.

TO MY FRIENDS:

SALLY SHARP, publisher, channel of the highest. Thank you for recognizing "Rosa." You always inspire me to reach higher with your love and joy.

PATSEY KAHMANN, editor, friend, healer. Thank you for always listening and knowing what I mean. It is wonderful to have someone who shares my hopes and believes in the importance of revealing the Truth. Your humor and empathy get me through the darkest hours of self-doubt and the pettiest of work that must be completed.

CRYSTAL ASHLEY, my courageous Firewalk partner. Thank you for your loyalty to the path of healing and for including me in the light of your angelic compassion.

CAROL DELONG-LOVELL, visionary. You don't know how beautiful you are! I am happy your vision of *Vows of Silence* has come true.

Thank you to the many friends who have crossed my path and all of the silent meditators, storytellers, lightworkers, healers, energy workers, starseeds, and hopegivers who are humbly and silently raising the vibrations of the Earth, accelerating peace and joy for all of Earth's inhabitants, in preparation for the Heaven on Earth to come.

Diana Louise Michael
May 21, 1993

INTRODUCTION

Religious beliefs killed
my mother and almost
destroyed me.

This true story
illustrates what harm can
come from the strict
interpretation and
propaganda of
religion—which is very
separate from God.

CHAPTER 1

"Scarlet Ribbons"

August 13, 1988

It's a Saturday morning. The dark cloudy sky is threatening a storm. A blessing after a hot summer drought. My husband Bill is out in the garage building railings for the new front porch he's adding to our rambler. Neva, our finch, is singing and swaying in her wooden cage in the living room. Flicka, a dead-grass colored Chesapeake Bay retriever, is in Bill's truck looking out the back of the topper pretending she's going somewhere.

Ken, my eighteen-year-old son, just came up from his room in the basement, where his walls are plastered with his drawings of rock stars, posters, and Minnesota-Twins-Win-the-World-Series memorabilia.

At breakfast, when I crack an egg open and slip it into the cinnamon muffin mix, I marvel at the double yoke. It is a twin egg—the most exciting event of the week. I thank God for that. Life wasn't always safe and uneventful.

Edward, my father, had been in love with Mom in high school, but marriage was not in my mother's plans at that time. My mom, Adelaide, went to nursing school in Chicago, while

Dad attended college in Wisconsin. After he graduated it was during the Depression and he was unable to get a teaching job, so he traveled with a big band, playing tuba and bass fiddle.

Being extremely private, my parents would never divulge to me what their social and love life was like during their twenties. My mother only alluded to the handsome doctors who wanted to date her when she was in nursing school. My father only talked about being a musician and never about any women he'd dated.

Eventually my mother's and father's paths crossed again and they were married. Mom quit nursing to start a family and Dad went into business, eventually managing a large advertising department in a major corporation.

By 1945 they had three sons. Mother had tumors in her uterus and doctors told her it was dangerous for her to have more children. Mom was a devout Catholic, who believed that God would make the decision whether she would have more children—whether she survived a pregnancy. Besides, she wanted a girl.

By January, 1947, she was pregnant with her fourth child. Mom was intelligent and sensitive, but she believed as she'd been taught that we were born to suffer and we were to offer that suffering up to God for entry into heaven. This simplistic, black-and-white, heaven-and-hell view of life prevailed in the forties and fifties. No one understood how powerful those beliefs were.

Mom lost weight during her pregnancy. On September 20th at 3:00 A.M. the doctor informed her, "You're going to have a stillbirth. We will have to induce labor. We detect no fetal heartbeat."

At 10:00 A.M. Mom delivered a living, three-pound baby girl. And twelve minutes later, expecting the afterbirth, she delivered me, a four-pound baby girl. Donna, my wombmate, was turning blue and I was bleeding from the ears. Mom hemorrhaged profusely and went into shock. My sister and I were put into incubators. The delivery room staff expected three fatalities that night.

As I grew up, my Aunt Cele often joked how little attention she had received in the hospital when she delivered my cousin, Danny, on September 19, because of all the attention the staff had given us.

Mother's doctor believed she needed an immediate hysterectomy, but due to blood loss, he felt she was too weak to survive surgery. But the hospital had a new miracle therapy—radiation!

No federal restrictions existed on the use of radiation in 1948—especially for use on a woman's organs. So they microwaved her uterus and ovaries.

When she recovered enough to see us, Mom performed a "civil baptism" to be sure we went to heaven; just in case the priest didn't arrive on time and we died with "original sin" on our souls. Catholic doctrine teaches that all souls are born with original sin on their souls because of the sins of Adam and Eve.

If a baby dies without baptism, which cleanses "original sin," its soul will not go to heaven but to limbo. If an adult who has been given a chance to redeem his or her soul through Jesus dies before being baptized, he or she could burn in eternal hell fire.

Catholics were given approval, if a priest were not present at a person's death, to perform a baptism themselves.

Fearing our death, mother saved us from limbo.

The overdose of radiation Mom received created havoc with the delicate balance of her endocrine system, causing a thyroid and hormonal imbalance that plunged her into a depression from which she would never recover.

Medicine did not have the knowledge nor the integrity to admit or correct its abuse. But it did have a candy-store galore of drugs to peddle to my mother. (Chemical dependency had not yet been recognized.) She was hooked on narcotics, amphetamines, and barbiturates that are now illegal and known to be harmful and addictive.

Mom was sent home from the hospital with her bag of prescription drugs to care for two premature infants and three small boys, ages four, five, and seven.

Although she gave us lots of hugs and affection, the constant telling of her medical horror story planted a message of guilt deep inside of me. It was all my fault—Mommy was sick because I was born!

CHAPTER 2

"How Much Is That Doggie In The Window?"

Once I believed that suffering was good, I was taught obedience—blind, unyielding obedience. One of the ways the Church ensured obedience was to make anger a sin.

When I was eight years old I began to question why grownups could get angry when I couldn't. Why they sinned, yet I could not. Adults didn't live by the rules they taught.

Sister Geraldine used to stand by the open doors of Blessed Sacrament School ringing a heavy brass bell as students filed in from recess. One morning a small black puppy scampered across the lawn and got in line with the students. Sister Geraldine yelled to the dog to "scat." When he came close to the doors, she hit him over the head with her bell. He fell, yelped in pain, and ran away.

In school when we had questions about life, we were always expected to consider what Jesus would do. I was taught to be a "soldier of Christ," to always be an example of Jesus on earth. I took this rule literally. I knew Jesus would not hit a puppy in the head with a bell. Why didn't Sister Geraldine know that?

As a child, I was always watching myself, always judging myself against the example of Jesus. By the age of six I already considered myself a dismal failure as a "soldier of

Christ." This belief made my childhood a living hell. I was never good enough for Jesus.

Adults do not realize that very young children trust them to tell the truth and believe what they are taught. In addition, a prevalent rule of the fifties was to keep secrets and pretend everything was wonderful, no matter how bad it got.

Authority was given further omnipotence in the cloak of a priest or nun who were said to represent God. I was totally vulnerable to the abuse of that authority. As a child, I was unable to tell when an adult gave orders that were not in my best interest. Because I feared authority and because I thought anger was a sin, I swallowed my anger and never learned to say no.

I was not only afraid of my own anger, I was terrified of anyone else's anger, especially my parents', who by commandment I had to honor. If an adult even frowned at me, my lower lip trembled. I was a quiet, obedient child. I felt responsible for my own bad feelings. I felt responsible for others' bad feelings, and I set out to keep people around me happy. Religion had taught me to get my good feelings from others, an early lesson that led to my victimization and enabling behavior, common issues of adults now.

As a child, I had no way of knowing that my father was overworked from having two jobs, supporting a large family, and having a chronically ill wife who never left the house and became more and more dependent on drugs.

When Dad was angry he slammed cupboard doors and rushed about the house not saying a word. I always thought I had done something to upset him.

He never outwardly got angry with us unless the toilet overflowed. All five of us became constipated fearing the bowl would overflow and Dad would come fuming through the house swinging the mop, cussing under his breath.

The overflow eventually destroyed the plaster on the ceiling below. One evening, Father Relic was visiting and we were all sitting in the dining room. Water started to drip from the crack in the ceiling above his head and over his glasses.

Dad suddenly realized what had happened and ran for the mop and into the silent upstairs where my brothers were hiding.

The rule that anger was a sin was a simple one. But the constant hidden messages about anger were confusing. The Bible story of Jesus getting angry at the money changers in the temple taught that anger was sometimes justified. But only for men. Anger was not tolerated in women and children.

This belief was constantly reinforced on television programs of the fifties. Even today, any woman knows an angry woman is labeled a "bitch." Women even call each other bitches. An angry child is labeled a "brat."

But what is an angry man labeled? A strong, masculine, virile hero. Men who do not display anger are called wimps or, worse yet, girls.

I believe this religious belief, supported by society, is responsible for the tolerance of physical and verbal abuse against women and children. Victims are still accused of "asking for it." Rendered silent by the law, anger is a sin—for women and children only.

Ironically, my father never expressed his anger directly toward my mother. My mother's anger about the past had turned into the only tolerated result of suppressed anger in women—physical illness. How could my father get angry with a sick woman? And so the denial that anyone was angry continued to keep our family silent, even though at times the anger felt suffocating.

The nuns and Mom often stated there was terrible evil in the world and things too horrible to talk about. And girls needed to be protected from the evil—whatever that was. Their strong message: the world was a terrible place and I was a weak sinner born to suffer in this world. And so, innocently enough, I had been taught that I had no control over my life.

Sadly, the institutions I learned to trust—marriage, religion, medicine, and the law—were the very systems that would endanger my sanity and my life. If only I had been taught to trust myself and know my own power.

Instead, I learned it was a virtue to suffer as Jesus

suffered in the crucifixion. I was encouraged to "find my cross." I memorized the rules, the catechism. I remember the words forty years later: "We were born to suffer in this world and be happy with God in the next."

I felt guilty for being happy because Jesus died on the cross for me. And because I believed my mother was sick and "dying" because of my birth, I was her cross to bear. I became my own worst enemy, sabotaging every opportunity to be happy or successful.

It wasn't so bad while I was segregated in parochial school and surrounded by children who believed suffering was good. But everything changed when I turned twelve and transferred to public school.

There I learned that not everyone believed in what the Catholic Church taught, not even most Catholics. To most teenagers I met, religion was a meaningless bore, a social hypocrisy forced on them by parents who wanted to impress the neighbors with their holiness. No one took it seriously except me.

I started to question the teacher at evening religion class and was told that we must accept everything the pope said as the truth handed down from God.

When I asked her why, then, had I been given a brain, she told me to ask a priest. The priest told me I must accept on faith, that it was a mystery. To keep me from questioning any more he told me that the devil was what made me question my religion. And so I quit going to religion classes. It held nothing for me but fear and oppression. But I kept asking God, believing God would not desert me for using the mind and heart I'd been given. Eventually, all the answers came in time and in ways I had never anticipated.

CHAPTER 3

"Mr. Sandman"

We lived in a big two-story brick and stucco house on a couple of acres of land on the East Side of St. Paul, Minnesota. Our house had a big living room with a fireplace. Attached to the living room was a sun porch full of windows that Mom used for a sewing room. A dining room and bathroom were adjacent to the small kitchen. The living room staircase wound up to four upstairs bedrooms. The full basement was big enough to roller skate in. There were corners, cubbyholes, pantries, and an attic just waiting for us to play hide-and-seek.

We were a ten-minute bus ride from downtown. My oldest brother still remembers the streetcars in St. Paul. He tells stories of the fun he had roaming in the tunnels underneath the trolley rails. I remember before I was six going downtown to shop at the Emporium with Mom. My sister and I weren't allowed to go downtown unless we dressed up in a skirt or dress. Sometimes we even wore our white Sunday gloves.

In the fifties, people could do with their land what they wished. The acre of land on the hill behind our house was undeveloped. My parents let my brothers and the neighbor boys put up forts on the hill. In one summer a small city of shacks sprouted up on the back hill: a tree house, a basement house, an earth-sheltered house in the side of the hill, and a few rickety, upright wooden shacks.

It was a time in American life that would disappear in the seventies when conformity, zoning codes, and fear of lawsuits would keep a kid's town like we had in our back yard from happening again.

Today that vacant lot is now a virgin woods in the center of the city. My dad hasn't sold out yet.

The boulevards of York Avenue were lined with giant elms that spread over the streets forming a canopy eight blocks deep, all the way from Case Street to White Bear Avenue.

In our yard three old elms guarded our house and provided shelter for squirrels and birds. Lush Boston ivy cooled the house all summer turning pear-yellow, fire-orange, and cranberry-red in autumn.

Next to our house was a valley thirty acres wide with a creek that twisted through the middle. The sumac were so tall you could hide under them. As a child my sister and I cut a hole through this "jungle" to get to school. It was an enchanted land. We knew we were almost on the other side of the "hole" when we heard the rooster crowing from the farm that faced Case Street. On the other side of Case, trains rolled over the hilly terrain shaking the windows in our house.

The family next door had a house on top of a big hill. In the winter we met the neighbor kids at the top with our sleds, saucers, and toboggans. We spent the winters sailing down the back hill that stretched a block long ending at a dirt road. Across the road was a haunted, abandoned house. We dared one another to go inside and up to the bedroom window, where the ghost had been seen. None of us ever made it more than halfway up the staircase.

In the summer the bottom of the hill became a baseball field. In the fall we were allowed to eat apples in a nearby orchard, but only the apples on the ground. We shook the branches with the best apples until they fell off the tree.

The good memories of childhood are just beginning to come back to me. Memories before Mom hid in the house. Before the drugs exalted her thoughts and bloated her body.

When I was a little girl I spent many happy hours in the

sand pile making mudpies and castles while Mommy sang hymns as she planted, dug, and pruned her terraced flower garden at the side of the house.

I can still see her dark, softly-curled hair pulled back from her face with combs, her long hair falling over her shoulders. She had bare feet and her patched jeans were rolled up above her ankles. Mom wore simple cotton blouses that hid her breasts, which were rather large for a woman who barely reached five feet tall and weighed little more than a hundred pounds. I constantly accused her of having candy in her shirt pocket. When I reached inside, there was none there. I couldn't figure out where the bumps came from. I thought she was playing a trick on me.

We stayed outside in the sand pile and garden until dusk when the sparrows came back to nest in the vines.

As I took my bath before bedtime, I listened to the sparrows chirping loudly outside the bathroom window. Summer mornings I woke up to the song of robins in the elm outside my window and the cooing of morning doves perched on the telephone wires that ran across the yard. I sometimes wished I were a bird. God took care of all the birds, even the scavengers.

I write this book from the suburbs, where miles of new developments are barren of trees. Where builders have thoughtlessly toppled acres of hundred-year-old oaks.

I realize now that as a child I was wordlessly nurtured by the presence of God outside my window at the same time words of religion were shouting sin, fear, and self-hatred inside my head, deafening the truth.

God was outside whispering—like the air—free, quiet, limitless, and always there.

CHAPTER 4

"I Say A Little Prayer"

When I left Blessed Sacrament School at age twelve, one nun I dearly missed was Sister Mary Patrick. She had treated me with affection and had chosen me out of her fourth grade class to place the crown of flowers on the statue of Mary at the May procession in front of the entire student body. When the chosen names from each class were put into a hat the principal drew my name.

I felt guilty that I had been chosen because of something shameful that had happened a few weeks earlier in church.

I was preparing my sins for confession and I had to go to the bathroom. No matter how hard I waved my hand, Sister Geraldine, the principal, ignored me. I was afraid to leave the church without permission. If I got up, everyone would look at me. I wished I was invisible.

I crossed my legs and prayed, asking God to help me hold it. By the time I got in line for confession my legs were trembling. When I finally got into the confessional I recited my list of sins as fast as I could. When I got to the one lie I had told, Father Relic stopped me and asked what I had lied about. Caught off guard, I explained to Father that I'd told my mom I vacuumed when I hadn't. My voice shook as I completed my confession, feeling a hot stream of urine run down my legs, soaking my white anklets.

When absolution was over I shamefully opened the

curtain, wondering who would kneel in the puddle I'd left behind on the kneeler. I knew I had to lie if anyone asked me if I did it. If I lied I'd have to find a way to go to confession before Sunday or I'd commit another sin going to communion with the lie on my soul.

As I knelt at the altar in front of everyone to say my penance, the prayers Father gave me to recite silently as punishment for my sins, I brushed my hand over the back of my uniform. I could feel it was damp and wrinkled. I wanted to run out of church, run far away, and never come back.

Before I finished saying my penance, I could hear the whispering of students behind me. I was sure they had discovered my secret.

Once I was back in school, two girls stopped me in the corridor. Shelly shouted, "Hey, you peed in the confessional. Didn't you?"

"No, I didn't. It was already there," I stammered, feeling my cheeks getting warm. My blushing face gave me away.

Of course, back then, it was the worst day of my life. The best day of my life in Catholic school was about to follow.

I remember the morning Sister told my classmates that I had been chosen to lead the May procession. Two girls who'd expected to win put their heads on their desks and started to sob. The girl behind me told her friend, "I can't believe she won. I was sure you would get it, Linda!" That week girls who had never talked to me before followed me around the playground. Other girls made loud remarks to their friends, making sure I heard. "She's not the prettiest." "She doesn't deserve it." "I hate sister Mary Patrick for picking her."

I hated it. I had learned a terrible lesson that week: that being successful meant girls would envy you, treat you badly, or be hurt because you beat them at something. Success meant to risk being disliked by anyone less successful.

As I grew up I started to feel that the one person I should never outdo and never be too happy in front of was my mother. How dare I be happy when she was dying?

By fearing others' disapproval, especially my mother's, I lost touch with my own needs. I didn't know my boundaries. I cared too much what others thought of me. I never learned to say no and followed a path that was not my own. I had learned my lesson too well. Insecure girls and petty women in authority began to manipulate me. The girl who would become my best friend was the most controlling of all.

The morning of the procession my sister left for school early to practice her Hail Mary recitation for the living rosary. Donna had been very quiet all week. She had been so excited about being in the living rosary until I told her I was going to lead the procession. I felt guilty again for being chosen.

I was tired the next morning from being up all night worrying. My mother dressed me in a wide skirt with a basket-of-flowers print, my white uniform blouse, and my first communion veil that had a high headpiece resembling the head of a Triceratops dinosaur.

As I walked to school the net insert in my starched slip made my legs itch. I was a walking umbrella. I fought back the tears. I didn't want to do this. No one liked me and I was sure I would forget to put the crown on at the right place in the hymn. And my parents weren't coming to church. Dad had a business appointment and Mom was sick. She was always sick! Why couldn't our family just be normal. I was angry at my mom and dad, but the shame and guilt I had learned for having feelings forced me to swallow my anger. Anger was a sin and deception was a sin. That left two options. Either stop feeling or deny your feelings.

Being an intensely emotional child, I could not shut off my feelings, so I chose denial! Only now do I see that my parents were acting out both those choices. My father, being more rational, chose to stop feeling. His calmness was something I envied. My mother kept feeling, and chose martyrdom. This was the model of the fifties. The Church had bred a generation of robots and martyrs. Following their parents, boys usually became robots, while girls became the martyrs.

The more I denied anger, the more frequently and vehemently I prayed, repeating over and over as I walked to school, "Honor thy Mother and thy Father." "Honor thy Mother and Father." I prayed constantly to keep the feelings, the sin, from coming out. On the outside I was a good, obedient girl who ate my peas, giggled easily, and never got angry. On the inside I was frightened of hell, confused about what my parents felt, and very, very sad.

When I arrived at school that morning Sister Mary Patrick said, "Come with me!" I followed her to the kitchen where students were forbidden to enter. She walked onto the green-and-white tiled floor over to the large, industrial-size refrigerator. I stood outside looking in, afraid to enter. Kids had been suspended for going in the kitchen.

"Come on, you humble little thing you!" Sister smiled and waved her hand at me to come in. "It's okay this time."

I timidly went over to Sister Mary Patrick. She opened the giant refrigerator door. I peeked inside. There on the metal shelf, next to a jumbo block of Velveeta cheese, was the Virgin Mary's crown, a delicate circle of baby's breath and pink tea roses just beginning to open.

I began the march from school carrying the delicate crown on a purple, velvet pillow. I led the students up the church steps and down the center aisle to the altar gate. A life-size statue of Mary had been moved from the school onto the altar. Mary had her hands stretched out in love to the world. The serpent Satan was wrapped around her porcelain feet. She had triumphed over evil. It was my job that day to represent the Virgin Mary. But I felt I was not worthy because I had peed in the confessional and lied about it.

I sat in the front row with Sister Mary Patrick and Sister Geraldine as the students sang hymns and recited the living rosary.

I carefully counted the hymns waiting for my cue. As the students sang "Hail Virgin Dearest Mary" I was to go up on the altar, climb the ladder in back of the statue, and carefully place the crown on Mary's head.

Everything went perfectly. I made it up the ladder without falling. I placed the crown on at the exact moment the voices sang, "....we haste to crown thee now." As I smiled triumphantly, the crown slipped down Mary's forehead and rested on her porcelain nose. The church echoed with laughter. My face felt hot as I looked down at the front row where the principal frowned at me. I reached in front of the statue to pull the crown up on Mary's head and lost my balance. A communal gasp let out from the crowd. I straightened my feet out without knocking over the statue and carefully balanced the crown on the top of Mary's head. The crowd sighed as I climbed down the ladder to the solid floor. I ran down the altar steps swinging my full skirt as I began the less than solemn march back to school feeling great relief that the May procession was over.

When I started attending public junior high, I still went to seven o'clock Mass before school. I prayed when I woke up and before I went to sleep at night. We had our own little altar at home in the upstairs hallway. There was a wooden prayer stand against the wall. Above it were statues of Jesus and Mary placed on half-circular wooden shelves hung from the wall. Inside the kneeler we stored our prayer books, hymnals, and rosary beads. Nearly thirty years later the statues are still there in vigil over my father's house.

At parochial school I'd been taught conflicting messages about the body. On the one hand, it was the temple of the Holy Ghost, and on the other, it was considered something to hide, bargain with, and ignore. Modesty was the word they used to induce shame. Even arms and ankles could be too seductive.

Since suffering was good, pain was good, so the longer you ignored physical pain, the holier you were. Why it was okay to do harm to your body (the temple of the Holy Ghost) was not to be questioned. The sins of the flesh were multiple. If you were concerned with how your body looked, you committed the sin of vanity. If you showed it naked, you committed the sin of immodesty. If you had pain, rather than considering it might be a warning your body needed attention, you were told to offer your suffering up to God, something my mother did daily.

By the time I entered junior high school my mother's health had deteriorated even more. She never left the house. For days at a time she did not leave her bedroom except to go to the bathroom. Years earlier my father had moved out of the master bedroom to share a room with my brothers.

Rumors spread about the woman that lived in the upstairs of our brick house. People had heard her singing hymns in Latin or sobbing from the window above the front door. We seldom had company in those years. I wonder now how my dad, a top executive in charge of a large advertising department, kept the secret of his hermit wife. As my mother's health deteriorated, he went on fewer business trips and came home for lunch more often to check on her.

I remember Dad most often wearing a gray suit, a white shirt, and a debonair hat, hiding his bald head. He wore wire-rimmed spectacles and changed to horned-rimmed frames in the sixties. Dad was always a devoted husband who drove up the driveway every night at exactly 5:30 P.M. without fail. He came in the house, set his briefcase by his corner desk, and put his topcoat and hat in the front closet. After he changed clothes and made dinner he did paperwork at his desk and was often still working when we went to bed.

Only as an adult could I comprehend what isolation he must have felt and what courage he had to be able to keep going with his wife hiding in the upstairs bedroom.

Anyone I ever met from Dad's work loved my dad! He was a different person at company picnics. He was sociable and outgoing and the first to laugh at the jokes. My friends all liked my dad, too. He was a gentleman. At home he was rushed and busy and seemed to be always saying, "Did you kids check on your mother?"

The doctors had freely prescribed barbiturates and Dexedrine (speed) for my mom and their effects on her motor skills and mental capacity were taking their toll. We lived in crisis.

She had been dying all my life. Her mood swings from the drugs were extreme. It became a family skill to go on with life amidst the erratic behavior of our mother, pretending that nothing was wrong.

There was a period when Mom collected rocks and wood. She gave us the rocks (some just from the back yard) and told us they were fossils hundreds of years old, or they had great gems hidden inside that we would inherit. I learned to keep a straight face when she gave me a rock. I would smile and thank her. I would add it to my small pile of rocks in the closet.

My family loved music. Before Dad married he'd been a full-time musician and played tuba and bass fiddle during the Big Band era. He liked Dixieland and jazz records. The turntable on our blonde-wood stereo console was always revolving. When we were very young Dad still played a couple of nights a week at the Friendship Club to supplement his salary.

My brothers were musicians in the school band and had hundreds of rock-and-roll records. In the early sixties they formed their own rock band called the Fortunes. My sister and our friends would sneak down the basement steps and watch them practice. My brother David became a professional guitarist and classical guitar teacher.

My mom loved Irish jigs and gospel music. She fashioned herself a drum out of a tin stool and a garbage can lid. She borrowed my brother's drumsticks and cymbal brushes, set up in the living room, and played the garbage can to her polka records. Other times when she was high on Dexedrine she played bongos in the basement between loading and unloading the laundry. When she was blue, Mom sang hymns in Latin. Whenever I hear Latin, the sad sound of her voice comes back to haunt me. The Mass had been traditionally said only in

Latin. Mom was furious when the Church changed the Mass to English.

Now I understand that the drugs she took were danger-ous narcotics, "uppers and downers." But in the 1950's, doctors were considered omnipotent and the pharmaceutical drugs they gave patients were legal. No one really understood then what damage they could do.

The top of Mom's headboard was filled with drugs, over-the-counter medicine, vitamins, rocks, and rosaries. She refused to go to the doctor. All she had to do was read about a new drug in her *Physician's Desk Reference* and call her friendly physician. He then called in the new prescription and Dad picked it up at the local drugstore every Friday. I loved to ride along because Dad would buy me a candy bar when he paid the druggist.

My Mom suffered from the radiation treatment. It had done its damage and the doctor tried to soothe Mom in any way he could. Back then the medical profession had little knowl-edge of the damage drugs did, or the addiction they caused.

In the fifties, chemically dependent people who were "caught" were labeled and incarcerated in mental wards along with the senile, retarded, epileptic, and every other kind of person society wanted to hide. People with any ailment medi-cine could not diagnose were put in the psychiatric ward, drugged, shocked, or brainwashed.

During one of Mom's highs, she developed a love for the color of metallic gold. Things started to disappear into the basement and return in the house with a shiny coat of gold spray paint. We had two gold rocking chairs, a gold waste basket, a gold stereo, and many gold rocks.

Mom had the Midas touch, everything she touched turned to gold. I still remember the discarded paint cans in the trash. We were the only family on the block with gold garbage.

I can smile now about the things Mom did when she was high, but this was the woman I modeled my life after. I was afraid I would go crazy, retreat to my bedroom, and never come out. How dare I be happy, succeed, and leave her behind! No wonder it would take me so long to grow up.

CHAPTER 5

"You'll Never Get To Heaven. . .if you break my heart"

     In 1962 I was transferred from parochial school to a public junior high school. For me it was like moving to a foreign country. Academics and morals, the keys at Catholic grade school, had no value in the eyes of my peers. The alien girls at the new school valued clothes and boys—in that order.

     What did I know about clothes after wearing a uniform since first grade? The nuns had drilled it into me, "To concern oneself with looks is a sin of vanity." My mother's wardrobe consisted of a closet-full of flannel nightgowns and jelly-stained robes. I stayed awake nights afraid other students would make fun of my clothes.

     After hiding in the house for so many years, Mother had no sense of how styles had changed. Montgomery Ward was her favorite designer. Wasting was a sin and recycling clothes a virtue. Because I was larger than my sister I was the lucky one to inherit my mother's hand-me-down clothes. Mom loved the song "Second Hand Rose." Her philosophy hasn't left me. My blood pressure increases at the glimpse of a clearance sale. Having was not for this life.

     Since I'd been nine years old I'd worn a holy scapular

around my neck. A scapular looked like two flat shoestrings
tied together with a piece of cloth the size of a postage stamp.
Imprinted on the cloth were pictures of St. Francis and St.
Christopher. The scapular had been blessed by the bishop. I
had never taken it off. It protected me from going to hell in
case I died in a car accident with a sin on my soul and hadn't
made it to confession on time. Of course, these were only the
venial sins, the smaller ones, like having impure thoughts or
saying bad words. Because in the Church, not only were
actions a sin, so were thoughts. More serious sins were mortal
sins. If you died without being absolved, your punishment was
eternal hell.

By the time I got to public school, the pictures had
worn off my scapular from wearing it all the time, even in the
bathtub.

On the first day at junior high school, I went to gym
class innocently wearing my scapular and my mother's hand-
me-down bra. As I walked into the locker room I saw girls
undressing in front of each other. And worse, they were laughing and talking as if they weren't doing anything bad. The
constant words of the nuns, "Immodesty is a sin" shouted from
the back of my brain. I sat down on a bench and debated
whether to walk out or stay in gym class.

The conflict I felt made me ill. I couldn't breathe. I
wanted to run away. My rigid beliefs had made an everyday
experience into a major crisis.

One girl who had huge breasts strutted around the room
showing off her flat stomach and narrow waist. When my stare
reached her face, I realized I had seen her before. Her name
was Shelly. She had attended the same parochial school as I
had. She was the one who had accused me of peeing in the
confessional.

Shelly laughed, and I was sure it was at my yellowed
hand-me-down bra. It was a horrible, long-line elastic thing
with stays on the side that dug into my skin and had hooks that
were difficult to unfasten. My mother didn't believe in wasting
anything and her old bras just happened to fit me. To get this

slingshot off, I had to turn the bra around to the front to unhook it, letting my breasts flop out in front of everyone. I was dying.

Then the gym teacher made me remove my sacred scapular before going into the swimming pool. By the time the communal shower had ended, my entire value system had been turned upside down. When I got back to my locker, my scapular was gone. I was ashamed. The poise of the other girls had made a mockery of my modesty. I didn't fit in.

Gradually, Shelly and I became friends. Even though I had not wanted to associate with her, we had one thing in common that drew us back together like magnets—parochial school. She was a spoiled child, always competing for attention. But like two aliens, we clung to each other for solace, making our way through the new planet—public junior high school.

She liked to control people. Being an obedient follower, I was soon believing everything Shelly told me. She proceeded to teach me her profound knowledge of life. Soon I had been told the horrible truth—in order to have children, men and women had to "touch down there."

The next time I went to church, I counted the people with children who had "touched down there."

I was aghast. Shelly liked to razz me about the fact that her parents only did it "once" because she was an only child, but mine must have "done it" at least four times. I was devastated. There was no way her dad, who drank liquor, who farted out loud and blamed others for it, could be holier than my father.

Mother, aware of my approaching womanhood, proceeded to tell me the Catholic doctrine of devotion to virginity that would save me from hell. She believed sex was only for "procreation," that God made it for having children. If she lived by that doctrine, she may truly have had sex with my father only as long as it took to endanger her life with her final pregnancy. Dad was as much of a saint as Mom was. In the early sixties, the Number One Rule was that a woman had to be a virgin to get married. And, unless she became a nun, a woman was expected to marry, or she was considered worthless. There were no other options. She could be oppressed by a husband or by a pope.

I had considered becoming a nun, but whenever I brought the subject up to my parents they ignored me. Besides, by age twelve, I already knew that I was too sinful to be worthy of being a "Bride of Christ," as nuns were called.

Virginity was what you traded for a husband. The final lesson was not only that the loss of virginity (for a girl) meant that no good man would marry you, but for me, it meant mortal sin and the loss of your soul.

The Church's belief in suffering took this a step further. Even if you lost your virginity by being raped, the girl was at fault. Ultimately, it would be better to let a man kill you than to rape you—to take away your worth—your virginity!

Mother constantly told me stories of saints who were dead virgins, saints who'd been slaughtered to save their virginity. They were heroines whose reward was to go straight to heaven. My mother's favorite saint was St. Lucy, who had beautiful eyes. In order to stop a suitor from pursuing her and risk losing her virginity, St. Lucy plucked her eyes out.

My mother had even convinced me to take Lucy as my confirmation name. I wanted the name of St. Rose, whom I admired, because she wore a crown of rose thorns pushed into her head. She was often depicted in a rose garden with blood trickling down her face, in honor of the crown of thorns of Jesus at the crucifixion.

The Catholic Church glorified the suffering and death of Jesus. The Church portrayed God the Father as cruel, petty, and merciless. By creating a tyrant God they bred a deep guilt and fear that kept people from leaving the "one true church."

I am a victim of that false witness. People tell me the Church has changed. But that won't resurrect my mother, nor the years I suffered because I believed as a good Catholic girl that I was my body and my body was dirty.

When I was fourteen I had a crush on a cute, blue-eyed blonde boy named Steve. He was in my journalism class. He had an animated face and told jokes that made me laugh and forget about my mom. I was lonely in high school and I dreamed about having a boyfriend. We had not been allowed to talk to boys in Catholic school. We had always been separated by sex. This created a mystique about boys that was unnatural. I imagined wonderful qualities in Steve that were not really there.

I even saved my money from babysitting to buy him a silver bracelet with his name engraved on it for his birthday. Shelly had been encouraging me to call him.

One night, after Steve had been out of school for two days, I dredged up enough nerve to call him. I thought he must be very sick because he had not missed a day of school yet that year. He'd never missed the Wednesday before the school paper was printed because he had his own sports by-line.

I almost fainted when Steve answered the phone. He told me that he'd missed school because his grandmother had died. We talked for over an hour. He was even nicer on the phone than he was in person. I'd never heard him talk seriously before without cracking a joke. At eleven o'clock Steve asked me if I'd meet him behind his house by the garage. Before he hung up he said, "You know, Di, you're a great listener." Without hesitating I agreed to rendezvous with him at precisely 11:35 P.M. It was my chance to give him the bracelet. I was so happy. He really liked me. He was so sensitive.

I wrapped up the bracelet with blue tissue paper, tied on a purple ribbon, and hurriedly dressed to meet Steve. I wore my red ski jacket over a sweater and jeans. It was nearly April. The outside temperature was only twenty-three degrees and it was snowing lightly when I quietly shut the front door behind me and crept down the front steps. Steve lived a half a mile from my house.

As I walked through the dark, empty streets, the wind boxed my face. I pulled the collar of my coat tightly over my ears. Hard, crusty mounds of dirty snow were piled high on the boulevards. I kept checking to be sure that Steve's gift hadn't fallen through the hole in my coat pocket.

As I came down the alley I saw Steve appear in the driveway behind his garage. He wasn't wearing a jacket. We talked outside for a few minutes. Steve rubbed his hands together and stomped his tennis shoes against the pavement trying to warm himself. He reached over and gently took my hand. "Let's go into the garage," he said. "I'm freezing. I'll show you my motorcycle."

Of course, I'd often seen him riding his gold metallic motorcycle the autumn before, and had wished he would invite me to ride on the back. But Steve didn't know I was alive. He opened the garage door. I followed him inside. I still remember the large oil stain on the concrete pavement next to his parent's car. The stain was in the shape of a body.

After showing me his bike, Steve started his parent's car, and turned the heater and radio on. I hopped inside on the passenger side and stayed by the door. My heart was pounding fast. What would I do if he tried to kiss me?

I took my coat off, set it over my lap, and took the gift out of my coat pocket and handed it to him.

He looked surprised when he opened it. "What's this for?" he asked.

"Your birthday!" I mumbled, feeling dumb. I knew his birthday had been over for two months.

"Thanks, I like it!" He took it out of the box and turned on the overhead light to see it better. "It's even engraved!" He leaned over and kissed me on the cheek. It was my first kiss. I was happy that he liked the bracelet. Embarrassed, I looked out of the car window at the floor of the garage. His hand brushed my leg as he moved as close as he could to me. He was no longer smiling. He grabbed my breasts with both hands and squeezed.

"Let go, you're hurting me!" I pulled away and reached for the door handle. "I have to go." I lifted up the door latch. Before I had the door open, he pulled me backwards and threw me against the steering wheel. "You do what I say!" he ordered in a violent voice that scared me.

I trembled and felt tears rush over my face. I choked back the sobs trying to hide my fear. I was dizzy and nauseated.

"Relax, you'll like it!" Steve came at me again.

"I have to go home now before my dad knows I left the house." I reached down for my jacket that had fallen on the floor of the car. Steve flipped open the glove compartment and took something out. When I sat up I saw he was holding the opened blade of a razor knife threateningly close to my neck. "Get your pants off!"

Without the word "No" in my Catholic vocabulary, I obeyed. But I wasn't moving fast enough for him so he angrily yanked my pants off the rest of the way. I shut my eyes. "Jesus, Mary, and Joseph. Jesus, Mary, and Joseph. Please, please, Jesus, Stop him!"

I waited for my guardian angel to rescue me—but she never came. When it was over a searing pain burned in my abdomen. I was bleeding. The knife was on the floor next to the gift wrapping. I was in shock. He had already dressed and left the car as I pulled on my clothes. My body hurt. I wasn't angry. I wasn't crying anymore. I was numb.

As I stepped out of the car a sharp pain shot through my groin. I wish he had killed me. This thought, like a bobber, kept floating up to the surface of my mind. I welcomed death to relieve the shame. How could I have been so stupid!

As I put on my coat and moved away from the garage he said in a shaky voice, "Don't you tell anyone, or else!" I couldn't talk. I started the walk home in the cold winter night. I had never felt so alone. Why didn't I just say "No"? Why didn't I let him kill me? My mother would have been happy. I'd have gone straight to heaven as a holy martyr. I'd be with Jesus and everything would be okay.

I had nothing left to save. Why should I continue to live? No man would want me now. I couldn't be a nun. I couldn't get married or have children.

As the snow whipped across my face I planned the next night to walk to the woods near our house into the hole and down to the creek. I'd take some pills and fall asleep. The snow would blanket my body. I'd fertilize the violets in the spring.

As I neared the house I wished my mother had told me what sex really was. Shelly was wrong! Steve had done a lot more than "touch down there." My God, I thought for the first time, what if I'm pregnant!

I stayed in bed for the next three days exhausted, depressed, suicidal. I told my parents and Shelly that I had the flu. I prayed for my period to come.

As awful as the rape had been, the worst violation was the lie of the Church, that I was only worth my virginity. I vowed never to tell a soul, not even Shelly nor my twin sister. I felt separated from my self and disassociated from reality. I had nothing left to save. I could no longer identify with any girls my age that I knew. They were virgins. When they pointed to other girls and whispered "whore" or "slut," they may as well have been pointing at me!

I was fourteen years old. The longer I kept the secret, the more suicidal I became. The guilt and shame would escalate into choices that would affect me for the next fifteen years.

When I returned to school I changed my pattern of walking to my classes to avoid Steve. I knew his class schedule by heart—so I went the opposite way and sometimes hid in the lavatory to be sure I wouldn't see him.

I asked the school counselor to get transferred from my journalism class. I couldn't stop crying in the office. There was no way the counselor could calm me down except by getting me a transfer. When he took me to the journalism teacher to get the transfer papers signed, I couldn't look in her face. The teacher knew that I loved journalism and wanted to be a reporter. She asked me why I wanted to get out of a class where I had received straight A's. I looked at the floor and didn't answer. "Please, God," I prayed. "Just get this over with before Steve comes to class."

I smiled gratefully the morning I woke up menstruating. Maybe God was still hearing my prayers. Getting my period was never so blissful as it had been that month. I promised God I would never complain about menstruation again.

I almost told Shelly about the rape when she badgered me to call up Steve and set up a double date with her and her boyfriend. She had the phone receiver in her hand when I stopped her.

"Don't you dare call him, Shelly! I mean it. I don't like him anymore! He's a slob!" Shelly's mouth opened wide with surprise. I had never raised my voice to her before. I wanted to tell her the truth, but I couldn't trust anyone with my secret.

"I hate boys. I never want to get married—unless I marry Fabian," I giggled, hoping she'd change the subject. (Fabian was a famous rock singer.)

Shelly laughed. "You're crazy. I'd rather marry James Dean than Fabian!" I breathed deeply, grateful that Shelly had dropped the idea of a double date with Steve.

"Let's go to the drugstore for a chocolate coke and onion rings!" Shelly went to get her coat. It was a cold April day with no sign of Spring. I put on my jacket and hurried to the door. "Let's go. I'm starved."

CHAPTER 6

"Please, Mr. Postman"

After the rape I kept to myself even more. I read a lot. *The Diary of Anne Frank* planted a seed of desire in me to write. I knew I'd never go through anything as profound as Anne Frank, but I was in hiding from the oppression of my given belief system.

My inability to relate to other teens made my loneliness more intense. I started to keep a diary. When I first began, I wrote pages for hours on end. When I'd read what I'd written I felt guilty about my anger with my parents and burned the notebooks I'd filled.

I started to write poetry. The following poem was written May 11, 1966, and shows the depth of confusion and despair I felt then.

> Wondering why I have
> no sweet expectation
> for something yet to come.
>
> Why does breath return
> each morning,
> my body to this tomb?
>
> When will breath be
> cause enough to join in joy of day
> When will I stop this bluff?

All my energies are pulled
and tugged by lives
whose trip would easier be lulled
were I not holding to survive.

Shelly and I became close friends. Almost weekly we
went on fasting diets together and then binged on ice cream
cones and chocolate chip cookies.

We had some foolish adventures, like climbing up the
concrete arches that spanned the side of the Robert Street
Bridge above the Mississippi River in downtown St. Paul. We
sat on the top of the fourteen-foot arch giggling as the drivers
passing below beeped their horns at us.

Our worst mistake was getting arrested for D.B.W.I.,
Driving Bike While Intoxicated. We were fifteen years old.

That sunny morning in late May I was home from
school, sick with asthma. I had taken ephedrine sulfate and was
resting when Shelly called me. She'd skipped school and asked
me if I wanted to run away. I told her I was too sick.

She persisted, persuading me to go to her house. I
obediently rode my twenty-four inch bicycle over to Shelly's
where we proceeded to explore her father's liquor cabinet.

I had never drunk alcohol before. We hated the taste, so
we opened beer bottles and emptied a third of the beer. Then
we poured in hard liquor, vodka, whiskey, rum, sloe gin. For
me the idea was to stop feeling anything. I wanted to experience an altered state of consciousness, one less painful.

We plugged our noses and chug-a-lugged the awful
concoction. At first I didn't feel anything. I remember after
about fifteen minutes I felt a hot fireball in my stomach and a
lightness in the center of my head, as the liquor combined with
the asthma medication I'd taken earlier.

We stacked rock-and-roll records on the turntable,
songs by Bryan Hyland, Bobby Vee, and the Beatles. We
danced through the house singing as loud as we could. Bootsie,
Shelly's Chihuahua barked and ran to his hiding place under

the kitchen table. We raided her parents' bedroom and blew up her father's condoms, letting them fly through the air in the living room, giggling as they deflated making a farting sound on their way to the floor.

By early afternoon we couldn't walk straight. We had to get out of there before Shelly's mom got home. We were going to run away on our twenty-four inch bikes—to California.

We slowly made our way to Maryland Avenue, so intoxicated that our bicycles occasionally meandered over the lane into the path of oncoming traffic. I'd forgotten my glasses at the house and was following the orange blur of Shelly's sweatshirt.

We got about a mile down Maryland Avenue when the light at the intersection of Arcade changed to red. Shelly zoomed across the street. I was nauseated and dizzy. I couldn't maneuver my bicycle around a parked car and get through before the light changed. My bike tipped over and I passed out on the sidewalk.

When I came to, there were shoes all around me. I heard a voice from a pair of red patent leather heels say, "She's drunk. I called the police right away."

The next thing I knew I was being lifted into the back seat of a patrol car. Shelly was already sitting on the other side of the seat. I do remember when I tried to get Shelly to talk to me that my hand accidentally brushed the arm of the police officer in the front seat. The officer angrily shoved me into the back seat yelling, "Don't ever touch a policeman!"

We were taken to the police station. As they wrote out the arrest papers, a reporter came into the station and took pictures. Luckily, they were not allowed to use them because we were minors. Shelly threw up in a wastebasket and I tried to hide under a wooden bench.

They transferred us to a detention center. We were searched, forced to wash in an open shower in front of two policewomen, and given worn clothes and the wrong size shoes to wear.

That night when Dad and Donna came to visit, Dad told

me that when the detention center informed him I was there, he told them they must have the wrong person. My sister told me it was reported on the television and in the newspaper that two girls were picked up for drunken driving on their bicycles. The reporters apparently cracked up laughing at the thought of it. But the detention center took their job very seriously. We were juvenile delinquents and they were going to shame us.

That night I was given a physical, including my first pelvic exam. The doctor was rough and hurried, pinching me with the speculum. He shook his head as though I were lying when I told him I had never drunk before. I cried myself to sleep in my locked cell that night. I learned the next day that Shelly's father had hired an attorney and she had been released the night before.

The next morning my father picked me up at the detention center and took me to the courthouse. I went to the court hearing wearing the jeans and sweatshirt I'd worn on my bicycle ride. Shelly came to the hearing with her parents and her lawyer. She was wearing a new pink outfit. They went into the judge's chambers behind closed doors. When Dad and I went in to talk to the judge he had already determined that I was the instigator.

I was given a year's probation and told to report downtown to a probation officer every week for the next year. Shelly received no probation. I was told that I had created a ruckus when I first got to the detention center, throwing the mattress on the floor and swearing—none of which I remembered.

The probation worker was stern and indifferent. In no way did she counsel me. I remember I had ironed a purple blouse and skirt before I went downtown on the bus for one session. When I got there she asked me why I didn't get my father to buy me some decent clothes. "He has enough money," she said. I had made such an effort to look nice. I was sure she didn't like me.

I didn't understand why she said my dad had money. Mom was always saying how poor we were, even though we had the biggest house on the block. Mom equated money with evil.

I hated going to that woman. I've often thought if I had been assigned a different probation officer, my entire life might have been different. I was ripe for intervention at that time.

I kept quiet and continued the weekly visits pretending I was happy and had learned my lesson.

It was not until the probation ended that my father learned the court files had been mixed up. A chart had been pulled for a girl named Diane who had the same last name as I had. The other Diane had done "everything in the book." God only knew what that meant.

Justice and the law were not synonymous. Shelly and I had committed the same act. I learned the law was political and money affected its decisions. It wouldn't be the last time that I would be harmed by the legal system. I had too little self-esteem to understand that maybe the system was at fault. I believed that I was bad. I was not only without my virginity, I was now a juvenile delinquent—a "J.D." they called us.

I also learned good looks and nice clothes, like Shelly had, made a difference in how people responded to you. Without a healthy mom to guide me and with the belief that vanity was sinful, I didn't know how to dress myself as a teenager.

I was overweight and had unruly, naturally curly hair. Straight hair was the *in* style of the sixties.

I tried everything to change my hair. I used a chemical straightener and bleached it blonde. I set it in orange juice cans and ironed it. I went on liquid diets to lose weight and fasted until my hands shook, and then overate and gained more back. Being a teenager was the worst time of my life!

There were nights when I sat in front of the TV fantasizing about how I would kill myself. On more than one occasion the only thing that saved my life was a celebrity on television named Steve Allen. His outrageous behavior made me laugh and forget my despair. I might be planning my method of death when Steve, wearing a Superman suit, would jump off a diving board into a vat of jello. You could hear his laughter echoing from inside the giant container as he climbed out, licking strawberry jello off his lips. As I watched him, I forgot to carry out my suicide plans. One night, I wrote Steve Allen a long letter, pouring my heart out.

I ran to the mailbox every day expecting a letter from Steve Allen. My brothers laughed at me. Even my dad told me, "Don't get your hopes up. You might get a form letter from his secretary, if you're lucky. He must get thousands of letters a week."

Dad could not have known "getting my hopes up" was a life and death matter.

It was shortly afterwards, early in December, 1964, when I took an overdose of aspirin.

I remember that I was given an assignment by my art teacher to design the backdrop for the set of the school play, *Oklahoma!* Although I was flattered, the memory of the rape haunted me. I didn't know how to accept this gift of trust from my art teacher.

I had some talent in art, particularly a good sense of color and balance, but I was too overwhelmed in the grief of losing my virginity to pursue anything. I thought my entire life was over. What was the purpose of going on? If I wasn't a virgin, I could never get married or be a nun.

After spending a week of nights in the basement filling sketchbooks with drawings of backdrops for *Oklahoma!* I became discouraged. I couldn't do it. Without another thought, I went to the medicine cabinet, turned on the water, filled a drinking glass, and swallowed fourteen aspirin. I screwed the cap back on the bottle and set the aspirin back in the cabinet.

When I came out of the bathroom, I looked at my mother. She was sitting on the sofa on a Dexedrine high mending holes in our socks. She had a wooden object, oval-shaped, with a handle called a "darning egg." It had strange letters embossed on it. S.M. Lucy. Mom moved the needle and thread swiftly back and forth across the darning egg.

Nobody I knew darned socks except my mother. For several minutes I sat across from her in Dad's recliner, watching her hands move and forgetting what I had done.

Dad was at the desk in the far corner paying bills. My brothers and my sister were not home.

I sat very still, relieved that I would not have to finish the art project because I would be dead in the morning.

But then I thought about Christmas. It was December. I looked out the living room window. It was snowing outside. Mom loved Christmas. It was the only time she believed in spending money. No expense was spared to celebrate Christ's birth.

I didn't want to ruin Christmas for everyone. I went over and stood in front of Mom.

She looked up and clucked her tongue, annoyed I had interrupted her darning.

"Did you finish your homework?" she asked.

"No. I.........I........I took some pills," I murmured.

"You *what*?"

"I took a bunch of aspirin," I said, looking down at my feet. Before I could say more, Mother was on her feet. She pulled her arm back and slapped me across the face.

"You ingrate! You are so lucky you have your health! What did you take?"

I started to sob and Dad ran over to see what was going on and to rescue me. My mother took some ephedrine sulfate, my asthma drug, out of her apron pocket and told me to take three, to counteract the sedative effect of the overdose.

As usual, I obeyed while Dad silently took my jacket and his overcoat out of the living room closet. Mother was shouting something out the front door at us, but we couldn't hear her. Dad drove down the driveway, leaving the garage door open.

I remembered Dad leaving the garage door open and knew it was a sign of his caring if I lived or not. He never left a door or window open or unlocked when he left the house.

Dad took me to St. John's Hospital to have my stomach pumped. There they tied my hands behind my back, secured me to a table, and forced a rubber tube down my throat. I gagged on the tube while they drained water into my stomach. I vomited as the doctor made a joke about my having had hamburger for supper.

They put me on a gurney in the corner of the emergency room behind a curtain for an hour and then sent me home. I received no counseling.

The next day I went back to school as if nothing had happened. When I got home my dad handed me an envelope that had arrived in the mail that afternoon. Inside was an autographed picture of Steve Allen and the following personal letter:

Twenty-Eighth
December
1 9 6 4

Dear Diana:

Thank you for your kind letter of December 8th.

You might be interested to know that my first reaction when you asked me to tell you about life was to make a note to send you my autobiography and then a paragraph later in your letter I discovered you had already read it.

Under separate cover I am sending you some of my other books. I don't really know how much they will teach you about life, but I hope at the very least they will suggest to you that it is well worth living.

I doubt if there is a person alive who has not asked himself at one time or another, whether life was really worth living. Therefore, you need not feel that you are unusual in that respect. Almost everyone, however, does conclude that life is indeed precious.

Write me another letter, a few months from now, and let me know how you are getting along and whether any of the ideas in the literature I am sending to you turned out to be helpful.

All good wishes.

Cordially,

Steve Allen

Only now, looking back, knowing how famous and in demand Steve Allen was, can I appreciate his response to me. In the years to follow, he wrote me many more letters and sent me his autographed books. Another mark of kindness and professionalism he showed was having his secretary write and assure me he had received my letters and inform me that he would be getting back to me when he returned from his travels. I now know this kind of compassionate response, considering the volume of mail he received, was phenomenal. Steve Allen had given me a priceless gift by letting me know that questioning the meaning of life was not unusual.

That summer I became a volunteer aide at a hospital for handicapped children. One morning when I went to work I found a ten-year-old girl on the ward lying in bed sobbing because she was no longer allowed to swim in the therapy pool. Candy had shiny black hair and beautiful brown eyes. She was paralyzed from the waist down. Her hands and feet had small stumps for fingers and toes. Her parents had given her up when she was a baby because of her handicap and she was made a ward of the state. Seeing Candy made me question why God would imprison this beautiful spirit in such a twisted body.

We became friends. I visited her on weekends and we played cards. She was not only beautiful, but smart and affectionate. At the end of the summer my asthma had gotten worse and I couldn't visit as often. When I did go back to visit Candy she asked me to adopt her. I was a suicidal sixteen-year-old, not much older than Candy, and she wanted me to be her mom! This dilemma added to my feeling of helplessness. I was too immature to visit her and remain detached. I loved her and had no way of helping her. I could barely help myself. The stress aggravated my asthma. I wrote Candy a letter telling her how I felt. I didn't think I'd ever see Candy again.

CHAPTER 7

"Michael, Row the Boat Ashore"

In my senior year at high school I went on a liquid diet. I hated it. It made me nervous and depressed. My hands shook. But I lost twenty pounds. And I saw a noticeable difference in the reaction of boys to me after I lost weight. That made me more depressed. One of the guys in English class patted me on the rear and said, "Hey, lookin' good!"

I'd been carefully taught not to value my body—but the outside world had a different value system. So I began to conform to the new value system of the new world I found myself in. But I was still play-acting. I was just beginning a search for new beliefs—beliefs that would release me from the guilt. I rarely stepped into church anymore, but the tapes still played in the recesses of my mind. "We are born to serve God in this world, and be happy with Him in the next!" "Life is suffering." "We all have our cross to bear."

I had to use any edge I could to feel more acceptable. I was frustrated because in real life looks mattered to other people and I'd been told they didn't matter. They shouldn't matter, but they affected everything. I even bought hard contact lenses so that I wouldn't have to wear glasses. Because I had allergies they were a constant irritant, but I refused to give them up.

I also noticed that ugly boys had girlfriends, but ugly girls did not have boyfriends. Nothing was fair. Becoming a nun looked more and more appealing. Then I could throw out the contacts, cut off my frizzy hair, and hide my body under a black dress. But, of course, I knew I was too unworthy for that because of the rape.

On our eighteenth birthday, my sister arranged a blind date for me with Michael, a friend of her boyfriend. Donna told me he'd been in our graduating class, but I didn't remember him by name. Over five hundred students were in our graduating class.

I spent hours getting ready for the big date. I redid my makeup three times, trying to contour my cheeks. I tried on five outfits before deciding on a soft rose-red sweater and black pants. I wore the perfume Dad had given me for my birthday. I had to smile at his choice of perfume. It was the only time I thought maybe he did have some insight into the personalities of his twin daughters. For me he had chosen "Ambush" and for Donna, "Taboo."

Michael arrived at 6:00 P.M. Dad called up the stairs to me, "Diana, there's someone here to see you!"

My heart skipped a beat as I came down the stairs, praying that he would like me. When I got down to the last step I gratefully watched Dad leave the room. Michael stood near Dad's desk. He had a stiff military posture. He walked over to me smiling and held his hand out to shake mine. "Hi, I'm Mike!"

"Hi." I shook his hand. "Donna and Dick have already gone to a show, I guess." I nervously looked down at the floor, impressed by the shine on Michael's polished brown boots. His tan pants were neatly creased.

Michael was cute. He had thick curly hair, even kinkier than mine. His eyes were slate blue—almost navy with flecks of yellow that softened his gaze. He had perfect teeth, small and even like rows of corn. A fading tan looked gold against the pale yellow of his shirt. Michael was easily taller than my dad, who was only five-foot-four. He appeared to be about five-eleven.

When I was calm enough to look at him again I remembered his face. "I know you. You were in my tenth grade English class."

"Was I?" Mike looked surprised and shrugged his shoulders. "I don't remember. English was my worst subject. Anyway, you want to go for pizza?" he asked.

"Yes, pizza's my favorite food!" Inside I was thinking I'd better not go off my diet.

I was surprised how comfortable I felt with Michael. He was so polite. He even opened the car door for me. On the way to Victorio's he told me about his family.

He had an older brother who was engaged to be married and moving out soon. His two younger sisters were in junior high school. His father was a retired policeman. Mike said his father had raised them alone since Mike was four years old. He didn't say what had happened to his mother.

After we settled into a secluded booth Mike ordered a large pepperoni-and-sausage pizza and a pitcher of beer. Alcohol had not touched my lips since the D.B.W.I. incident. Mike must have seen the uncertainty on my face.

"It's only 3.2," he said. "You want something else?"

"No, I'll have a beer." I said. "Just one." By the time we lifted the pieces of pizza off the pan our serious conversation had turned to giggles. We were laughing at each other as we tried to flip the long strings of mozzarella hanging from the pizza into our mouths. Michael's full lips were shiny with sausage grease.

Without thought I said to Michael, "You have nice lips."

Michael's face turned red. Without warning he reached over, lifted my hand, and kissed it. "You're sweet!" he said.

I could feel a blush warm up my face. He was so nice!

We talked in the red vinyl booth for hours. Tears came into Michael's eyes when he told me about his dog Jody. "She's got bleeding ulcers in her stomach. The vet says I'm going to have to put her to sleep." I took ahold of Michael's hand. He affectionately squeezed my fingers.

We hadn't noticed the other customers leave. Finally I realized the waitress was cleaning off the tables. She kept looking over at us checking her watch. Mike stood up, took his wallet out of his back pocket and threw a ten-dollar bill on the table. "I'll be right out." He disappeared into the "Gents" room at the back of the restaurant.

I liked him. But he had no idea what turmoil was going on inside of me. I would hide my fear of life as long as I could. I didn't want the night to end. It seemed so simple—suddenly Michael was all that mattered. I didn't want to go back to the house and hear my mother singing Gregorian chants. I wanted Michael to gently touch my hand again and tell me I was sweet. I was thirsty for the kindness he showed me.

When the moonlit night was over, Michael walked me slowly up the sidewalk to the front door. The porch light was on. The damp autumn leaves clung to our shoes. "Thank you," I said. "I had fun."

"Me, too." Michael started to zip up his windbreaker. I put my arms around him and held him as tight as I could, pressing my face against his chest. He stood still. I heard his heart beating as his hands caressed my hair. He was so warm. He pulled me closer. A circular motion stirred in my heart, opening like a flower to the morning sun. Was this love?

"When can I see you again?" he quietly asked.

"Come back in an hour!" I said into his shirt, afraid if I let go he'd be gone forever.

"Hey," Michael lifted my chin up. He must have seen the fear in my eyes. "I'm coming back, you know."

I let go of him, thinking how desperate I must have appeared.

"I'll call you tomorrow." He walked to the car. "Dick gave me your number," he yelled to me.

"What time?" he shouted from the street. "What time should I call you?"

"Anytime after 4:30 is fine," I shouted back and waved. "Good night. Thanks."

"See you tomorrow!" He waved as he got into his car.

When I shut the door I smiled. It had been a wonderful date. Even if he didn't call back.

But Michael did call and after that night Michael and I became a couple.

After dates we went to a private place down a secluded dirt road that lead behind Big Sandy, a hill by the railroad tracks. We talked and joked and tickled each other. We kissed and held one another—with our clothes on.

There were times we lost control and started to undress—but I told Michael I was afraid of getting pregnant. He accepted that. I thought he would be able to tell physically that I wasn't a virgin. The more we held back, the more excited we became. It didn't really matter that our clothes were on. I would straddle Michael, placing my knees at each side of his thighs. We fondled and rubbed against each other, getting so excited we finally climaxed together.

Touching with love was magic. I didn't feel alone when I was wrapped in Michael's arms. Being loved by Michael had nothing to do with the violation I had felt when I was raped.

The more I experienced my sexual feelings, the angrier I became that I had been lied to. The Church had taught that sex was dirty—period. A sin out of marriage—a duty in marriage. Where did the affection and pleasure I felt with Michael fit in? Maybe the world didn't validate our love, but God knew what was in our hearts.

I began to realize that what I *felt* was what would lead me in the direction that was best for me. Not what others had told me. Maybe suffering was right for my mother, but it was not what I wanted for the rest of my life.

There was a silent voice that knew its direction. God had given animals an endless trust, an instinct for survival. Would God deny us the same gift? It was difficult to listen to a voice as quiet as the sun, when the world had taught us to make every decision based on fear. "You'd better get insurance

because something bad is bound to happen!" "You'd better
build a bomb shelter because the Communists are coming." For
years when the air raid signal screamed its monthly warning,
I'd hide on the porch behind the Singer sewing machine. But
the Russians never came. I'd been taught to cower and prepare
to be a victim of evil. I'd learned my lesson well. It would take
so long to learn the evil was not Satan, nor the Russians, but
my own fear.

When would I learn that we are always safe? We live in
the Heart of God.
Being in Michael's arms felt safe to me. He taught me
how to love. The only problem was, I didn't love myself yet.

Nineteenth
July
1 9 6 6

Dear Diana:

Please forgive me for having taken so long to respond to your letter of June
28th. One of the pleasant things about working on television is that you
receive hundreds of letters each week. Answering that many letters, of
course, is something else again.

Quite a lot of the mail can naturally be handled by form-letters written and
signed by members of our secretarial staff. But the important letters, such as
yours, I insist on answering myself. The only problem is that there are just
24 hours in a day and therefore I am frequently late in responding.

At this great distance, and having no real knowledge of your situation, there
is not a great deal that I can suggest, but I can, I think, make a few general
observations that might possibly be helpful to you.

The first thought is that while you may have more than your share of misery
and suffering, nevertheless everyone who has ever lived feels this deep
depression at one time or another. As I look back over my own teen-age
years, I think I spent more time being miserable than I did enjoying myself.
But I learned early in life that no matter how unhappy I felt at any given

moment, there was always a swing of the pendulum before very long so that over the long haul, some sort of balance was achieved.

My second suggestion is that you must at your earliest opportunity seek professional counsel. None of us -- however wise -- is strong enough to deal unaided with his own serious emotional problems. In fact, when psychiatrists and psychoanalysts themselves have serious problems, they do not treat themselves but seek the professional services of one of their colleagues, just as dentists and other doctors do.

You are very wise to perceive that you are the one that must change if your life is to become a happier one. This is not to say, of course, that you are the cause of all your own troubles. Very often overly sensitive people suffer needlessly because of the thoughtlessness of those with whom they must live or work.

Having had the unfortunate experience with the overdose which your letter explains, I am reasonably certain you would not be so unwise as to attempt to take this way out again. You are most intelligent in realizing that your true purpose was not to end your life but to make others pay thoughtful attention to it.

As regards some of the philosophical questions that are troubling you, you need not be unduly dismayed by your inability to resolve them with any degree of finality. A number of them are unanswerable in this way, in the sense that a problem in mathematics or physics is answerable. As regards the existence of God, for example, I accept it largely because the opposite alternative seems even more preposterous. But it is difficult indeed to retain one's faith in a world in which so much injustice and suffering is common. Since you are kind enough to compliment the other books I sent you, I am enclosing my latest, which deals with one example of the injustice and suffering to which I refer. It is called "The Ground Is Our Table" and deals with the plight of our nation's migrant farm-laborers.

Oh. . .one last suggestion: it sometimes is helpful to have something outside of yourself on which to concentrate, perhaps some worthy social cause or charitable movement. I'm sure that in the fine city of St. Paul there are many organizations that would be glad to have one additional energetic volunteer.

All good wishes to you.

Cordially yours,

Steve Allen

That Fall I attended the University of Minnesota. Michael worked days as a car mechanic. At school I was lost in the mass of forty thousand students. My friend Shelly and I had drifted apart. She was busy planning her wedding. My depression eased after Michael. I had a boyfriend. I finally fit in.

At the time I was questioning life, two of my brothers had joined the Transcendental Meditation movement. They planned to go to India and become TM teachers, bringing the meditation tradition to Minnesota. The Beatles and Mia Farrow had started Transcendental Meditation, making it a famous practice.

I didn't understand what TM was at the time, but I was impressed with Maharishi Mahesh, the yogi who was happy. No matter how reporters maligned him, no matter how much ignorance and bigotry were aimed at his culturally different dress and speech, he always made light of it in dignity and humility. Less spiritual gurus would ride to power on the wave of his accomplishments. And some of those who would practice TM would commercialize the tradition.

Inside I began to measure the value of a person's beliefs by how happy they were, rather than by the material and social values of society. This internal change created a greater chasm in my search for an identity because the world only believed in the external markers of success. I was taught the "kingdom of God is within," but it took an Eastern monk to teach me how to know the Christ inside, by stilling my mind in meditation.

I had finally accepted questioning, no longer fearful of the gift of mind I'd been given. But I was a long way from knowing discernment. Having been taught that I had no value as an individual or a woman, I had learned to trust everyone but myself. I assumed everyone knew more than I did. I was open to whatever floated my way. Everything—whether wise or foolish.

I wanted to run away with Michael, get married, and start a new life away from the tragedy of my dying mother. The closer Michael and I became, the stronger my fear was that Michael would discover I was not a virgin.

It was the Spring of 1967 when the tightly knit security of our relationship began to unravel.

I was going to school. Dad was willing to pay for the whole thing. But emotionally my thoughts were scattered. I ruminated about the meaning of life and the purpose of going on with it. I was not able to cope with the anonymity of a large university, nor the demands of studying. I had writing talent and an opportunity to major in journalism, but my grades were barely passing, adding a feeling of failure to my depression. My only chance for an education was fading before my eyes. My mind hovered like a twirling top, ready to topple at the slightest touch.

I wanted to quit and get a job, have some money like my sister. But I didn't know how to tell my father. If I quit, I would never get my degree. I wanted help, but I didn't know where to go.

I went for long walks and tried to sort out my life, but I was too depressed to make any sense of it. I sometimes stood against the railing on the Washington Avenue Bridge watching the swirling water of the Mississippi pass underneath—and thought of jumping off.

I went to my college advisor. He told me frankly that I might as well quit and get married—that degrees were wasted on women, who only came to college to get husbands. He didn't know that I was not a virgin and that marriage was not an option for me. I was Nobody to him. I didn't belong at college. I was invisible there. Confusion turned to despair.

Michael didn't understand my constant questioning. He lived to work on his car and play with his new golden retriever puppy, Buck. Life was simple. Michael sometimes fought with his dad, who wanted Mike to become a man by joining the service or the police force. Most of the time Michael was happy just to have a spaghetti dinner, a dish of spumoni ice cream, and a hug and a kiss from his girl. Sometimes he joked about getting married and having a "little one." To me it was only a fantasy I could hold onto until he found out I wasn't a virgin.

My hair had grown long. The weight of it softened the curl. Michael liked it. I was going to have it done at the beauty parlor for Shelly's wedding. I wanted to wear it up in puffy curls called "love locks."

Shelly attended beauty school to become a hairdresser. She agreed to touch up the dark roots of my blonde hair before her wedding.

She applied the chemical dye she'd picked up from school and wrapped my hair in plastic. Shelly and I visited while we waited for the rinse to set. She forgot to set the timer. Thirty minutes later she removed the wrapping and rinsed the foam off. When I saw the look of horror on her face I ran into the bathroom to look in the mirror. My entire head of hair, except a half-inch of growth at the root, was army green.

I immediately called my dad. He took me to the beauty salon. They tried to cover it with black dye, but it wouldn't cover the green. The beautician said I had been lucky that my hair didn't fall out. She told me that anyone knows from the first week of beauty school that if bleach is mixed with a rinse a person's hair will turn green.

The beautician cut off my long hair. I came out of the salon with a half-inch of black hair, looking like a prisoner of war—except for my gopher cheeks. I was so ashamed I hid from Michael, my only support.

I never returned his phone calls. He came to our house twice, but I persuaded my sister to tell him I wasn't home. I was so afraid he would reject me, I rejected him first.

That Fall I suffered miserably from a hay fever allergy. The drainage caused lung congestion and I had asthma. The ephedrine sulfate I was taking relaxed the bronchial tubes and allowed me to breathe easier. In fear of having an asthma attack I started to self-medicate, taking a pill at the slightest tightness in my chest, with the first wheeze.

I fasted to lose weight, increasing the effect of the drug in my system. My hands visibly shook. I lost sleep, became anxious, irritable, and paranoid. I was feeling disoriented and shaky. I had trouble listening to my teachers. I missed Michael.

Most days I just wandered the campus ruminating about my purpose in life.

In one of my classes, the teacher was dividing the class into two groups, a "speaking group" and a "writing group." That day the teacher brought me out of my reverie, pointing at me with his ball-point pen. "You're talking," he said. Then he pointed to the guy next to me.

I stood up and yelled, "I was not talking!" Then, realizing suddenly that he was only choosing me for the "speaking group," I ran out of the room and went into the lavatory and hid in the stall, lifting my legs up so no one saw my feet.

I cried until the tears dried up, praying no one would come and find me, secretly wishing someone cared enough to do so.

I walked to the Washington Avenue Bridge over the Mississippi River and looked down at the water churning below. I felt like jumping into the waves, ending my confusion.

Losing track of time, I eventually walked to the bus stop and took a bus west to a walk-in clinic where I asked for help.

CHAPTER 8

"Help"

Before I was spoken to at the clinic, I was given a battery of tests with some odd questions, like "Do you hear voices?" One of the questions asked about riding on a streetcar. There had been no streetcars in St. Paul for twenty years. Some even asked about bowel movements and bathroom habits. In the group of possible answers none could be unequivocally true, making it impossible to be honest. After the test I was sent on my way. No one would be able to see me until the tests were scored and returned in a week. I doubted if I would live that long.

Somehow the anticipation of help kept me going for another week. When I returned to the clinic I was advised that being locked in a hospital ward for a month would be the best thing for me. They told me my father's insurance company would cover the stay. I obediently went home and packed my suitcase. I wrote a long love letter to Michael and mailed it on my way to the bus stop. I remember riding on the bus with my suitcase, feeling like a runaway. I told no one where I was going. I would let the hospital call my dad.

I was taken up to a locked station and shown the room I would share with a girl named Terri. Before I unpacked, the nurse gave me two orange Thorazine tablets. She was in charge of my being medicated four times a day. My roommate had warned me that I might gain weight on the tranquilizers. Terri was hospitalized with hysterical paralysis. Her hand was closed into a fist.

By the third day on the drugs my mouth was so parched my lips stuck together. I could hardly talk. My vision was blurred. I couldn't read because the letters all ran together. I felt lethargic and my weight dropped. Within two weeks I'd lost seventeen pounds from dehydration. I was not having a normal reaction to the drug, but no one did anything about it. I was a zombie. The psychiatrist I had trusted at the clinic was not the psychiatrist they assigned me in the hospital. By the time the psychiatric intern came to see me I was nearly incoherent. She was a short, mannish woman with hair the color of a rodent. Her pasty face was emotionless. Her voice, matter-of-fact. She came daily and asked, "How are you today?" When I responded, she squinted her eyes and slowly made notes in my chart, not saying another word. When she was finished charting, she left abruptly, never giving me any indication of how I was doing, nor what was expected of me except obedience, at which I was an expert.

None of the issues surrounding my depression were addressed: not religion, not my mother, not my family, not my values, and never my beliefs. I guess I was sure they would just figure this out by magic. Daily I dressed, exercised, ate, and attended group therapy. I made friends with the patients. There was a young man named Lawrence who wore thick glasses and was facing inevitable blindness. My roommate Terri was receiving hypnotherapy to discover why her hand was paralyzed. They could find no physical cause. Ironically, I learned that she'd been brought up Catholic and aspired to be a nun. It was discovered through hypnosis that she believed that it was evil to be touched, especially if you were going to be a "Bride of Christ." Those beliefs preceded the paralysis. At a family gathering, a relative had held her hand. It folded up and never opened again. Blessed with a more progressive doctor than I had, Terri was treated with hypnotherapy and she subconsciously began to loosen her rigid beliefs. We celebrated the night she moved her little finger.

One patient had migraines. She received electro-shock therapy. Another was anorexic. They put her in isolation when she refused to eat. I was fascinated with a Cuban woman named Shalimar. She had long black hair, large green eyes, wore heavy makeup and false eyelashes, and dressed with plunging necklines, exposing her huge melon breasts. I didn't know why she was in the hospital. Everyone whispered about her the night two policemen visited Shalimar's room.

Another patient who intrigued me was an overweight man named Lee. He was articulate and outspoken in group therapy. He wore clear nail polish on his long, sculpted nails.

One day I walked by his room and saw a visitor—a stocky blonde wearing a blue suit, fluffy white blouse, and high heels. When I told Terri to go by Lee's room and see his wife, she said, "That's not Lee's wife. That's Lee." I still didn't understand. A year later I would learn what Shalimar and Lee had in common.

At the end of four weeks, any healing I'd received was from the other patients who cared about me and wanted me to live.

Without warning they took me into an office to see a doctor I'd never met and informed me that my dad's insurance coverage had ended, so I would be released from the hospital that day with a supply of drugs. But the "good news" was that they had a "wonderful opportunity" for me. A beneficent director of a nursing home in the suburbs had a program for girls "like me" where I could get "free" room and board by working as a nurse's aide.

When I arrived at the nursing home with my suitcases, I was surprised to enter a clean, plushly carpeted mansion. As we went through the corridor I saw the patients' rooms were well-lit and pleasant.

As we walked further down the long hall a young girl about thirteen rolled her wheelchair out of her room into the corridor. It was Candy, the girl from the children's hospital who had asked me to adopt her four years earlier.

I wasn't sure if she recognized me. I had short dark hair and was thin from my reaction to the medication. What was she doing in a nursing home with the sick and dying?

That evening I met the other women warehoused in the room with me. They were totally dependent on the nursing home. June was a paraplegic. Maureen had been mentally ill for fifteen years. Cheryl was severely retarded, obese, and wore glasses with thick lenses. And Ann, a tiny woman no more than four feet tall, had one eye and a club foot.

In return for my six-by-five-foot space, I got up at 6:00 A.M., worked as a nurse's aide for eight hours a day, and ate leftovers from the kitchen after the patients had been fed. I could run away but I had no idea how to get home. Each morning I woke up to Ann's alarm and the sound of her foot dragging across the floor as she dressed for work. She, too, had to work a full day for her room and board.

Frightened of being doped up, I stopped taking the tranquilizers and hid them in the zippered pocket of my suitcase. As my body adjusted and returned to "normal" my clear vision returned. I became alert and aware for the first time since my hospitalization.

Candy and I played cards together in the lobby evenings. Neither of us mentioned the past.

Every day I bathed Myrtle, one of the more fragile elderly women. She knew me and smiled when I came into the room. Every day when I was finished washing her, she pointed a shaky finger at her night stand. "Have a cookie. They're lemon. My daughter brought them but I can't eat them because my teeth don't fit, dear." She smiled a toothless grin.

I patted her weathered hand, speckled with liver spots and blue-swelled veins. I took one lemon cookie and thanked her. I loved Myrtle.

One morning as I was looking out the window while I started to run the bath water, I noticed a hearse outside. I ran down the hall to Myrtle's room. She was gone. Her bed had already been stripped and prepared for another person. Stricken with grief, all I could think of was how my doctor could believe this place would make me want to live.

The third week of my stay, while sitting in a high-backed chair in the lounge reading, I overheard the nurse talking with an orderly. "Diana is doing so well. She's the first schizophrenic we've had here!"

My heart thumped wildly with fear. Schizophrenic! I had to get out of here. I was depressed, but I wasn't delusional. She'd only seen me in the zombie state I'd been in from my abnormal reaction to the Thorazine that she'd prescribed. I was eighteen and had been placed in a room with four women whom society had disposed of.*

If the nursing home administrator discovered I had stopped taking the pills, the nurse could inject me with Thorazine. I'd seen people in the hospital restrained and drugged when they didn't cooperate. I'd be a zombie again and never get out!

I stood and walked down the hall, praying the nurse would not notice me. I got to my room, put on my coat, and ran out the back exit. I walked as fast as I could to the closest phone booth and called Dad at work. "Please, please, you've got to come and get me. Please, right away. I'm scared." Tears ran over my face. I begged, "They said I was schizoid. Why didn't you tell me? I'm not paranoid. I'm not." I listened intently while watching to see if anyone from the nursing home would come and find me.

"I have to finish up some work here before I leave. It'll take me at least an hour to get there. Does the doctor know about this?"

"No, Dad, don't call the doctor, please! I'm not going back there. I'm at the gas station at the corner. I'll wait here for you. Please hurry!" When I got off the phone, I called Michael. He answered the phone right away. I sobbed between words. "Michael .... Michael .... This is Diana."

When I told him where I was he did not hesitate. "I'll be

right there!" He hung up before I could tell him that Dad was
on his way to get me. I remembered how I loved Michael. I
decided that moment I was going to marry him.

*In the sixties, schizophrenia was a common misdiagnosis used for many
disorders in a medical system, just like today's, that had to label patients to
expedite billing. The practice of making a rushed diagnosis for financial
reasons is still prevalent in many mental health settings because it is
mandated by the insurance company. For patients it can be a life sentence
that destroys their credibility, no matter how well they might become.

Even for those who are delusional, with symptoms warranting a
diagnosis, a new mental health terminology would be beneficial. In the
same way that words once commonly used in psychiatric wards, such as
imbecile, feeble-minded, idiot, and moron have become obsolete, other
derogatory absolute labels still existing might one day be changed to benefit
patients' upgraded recovery.

CHAPTER 9

"Soldier Boy"

I'd returned home determined to go on with my life and forget the past, but the negative messages given to me by the "experts" left their mark. Ironically, the people I'd gone to for help had seen me as "hopeless," damaging my self-esteem further. I tried to ignore their opinions and force myself up again.

Michael came back to me. I'd been so stupid. He didn't care that my hair was cut short. He didn't care that I'd been in the hospital. He still loved me.

I got a job as a nurse's aide at a hospital working in the nursery. After the babies were delivered, I washed, weighed, and measured them. I rolled their tiny feet on ink pads and stamped their footprints on birth certificates. I changed diapers and bottle-fed newborns.

The sense of joy I felt seeing new life after being in the home of the "dying" was a healing experience for me. This job was the first success experience I'd had since being chosen to crown the statue of Mary at the May procession.

I'd learned to keep my mouth shut about my depression, my mother, and my religion, pretending to be normal, fearing I was crazy.

To the staff I was just another carefree teenager, but inside I lived in fear they would find out I was labeled and get rid of me. Of course, the word of a psychiatrist was infallible, and the word of a teenager invalid.

I know now that I am highly suggestible and can be hypnotized at the slightest command. This explains why I was particularly vulnerable to the authoritarian doctrine of the Catholic Church and the psychiatric diagnosis made while I was heavily drugged. Empathy is the positive side of my suggestible nature, but I learned the hard way that having empathy without discernment can lead to self-destruction. Being born female, I'd been taught to deny my own feelings in the service of others. My sense of rational judgment was not developed and my overly suggestible nature made me open to whatever suggestions I was given.

I stopped questioning life and concentrated on loving Michael, dreaming of marriage and of having a baby. After we were reunited I wanted to make love to Michael, but the old fear of him knowing I was not a virgin resurfaced.

One weekend in early Spring Michael's dad and sisters went out of town to visit relatives. Michael had to work that weekend so he couldn't go with them. He and I went out for pizza Friday night and went back to his house.

I sat on the sofa while Michael searched for a cork-screw in the kitchen. After a noisy search through the drawer and muffled swearing, he reappeared with a bottle of wine and two crystal wine goblets. He poured slowly and handed me a full glass. In a toast he touched the rim of his glass to mine, "To our love! Forever!" We stared into each other's eyes as we sipped the rose wine. Before the glasses were empty I was lying on top of Michael on the sofa.

Through the clothes I could feel him throbbing against me. I kissed his eyes. I touched his hair, his face, his lips.... He suggestively darted his tongue in my mouth, sending a signal through my body. Playfully responding, I thrust my tongue through his closed lips.

Michael gently unhooked my bra and cupped my breasts in his warm hands. We silently lifted ourselves off the sofa and hand-in-hand walked upstairs to his bedroom. I was ready when he entered me for the first time. He was slow, warm, and pleasure-giving. I felt the thrill of orgasms rising through my body in waves.

The second time we touched each other in the darkness, learning what gave one another pleasure. It was new again! We slept in each other's embrace and woke later that night to love each other again.

"I don't want this to ever end!" he whispered as he kissed my face.

"I don't either." I held his hand. "Right now I could die happy!"

Half-asleep, I rested my face on Michael's chest. Suddenly overcome with emotion, I began to sob.

"What's the matter?" Michael caressed my hair. "Did I hurt you? Are you okay?"

"No, no. It's not that." I turned to face him. "It's not you."

"What is it?" Michael sat up.

"I'm afraid to tell you. You'll hate me!"

"I won't, Diana. Nothing could make me hate you. Nothing!" Michael took my hand. "Tell me."

"I was raped when I was fourteen by a boy I knew." I wiped the tears away.

"He...he had a knife...so I let him! I was so stupid!"

Michael got up and put on his clothes.

"Are you angry?" I asked as I pulled my sweater over my head.

"No, no, of course not, not with you! But I'd like to kill the son-of-a-bitch who did it! Do I know him? Did he go to our school?"

"Yes. But I thought he was nice. I never really knew him. What bothers me is, how many other girls has he done it to since then? I never told anyone but you."

"Didn't you even tell Donna or your mom?" Michael came up behind me, held me and rocked me in his arms.

"How could I? It's a mortal sin. I should have let him kill me! Then my mom would be happy. I'd have been a saint, a martyr. I'd sit at the right hand of God and nobody would think I was bad or crazy."

"Hey," Michael turned me around and kissed me.

"You're not bad or crazy. Who cares what they think anyway?"

"You're Catholic, Mike. How can you say that?" I pulled away and sat down on the bed.

"My dad and mom are divorced!" He sat down on the bed next to me. "I don't believe in half the shit they teach you. I hardly remember my mom. I wish my dad would find someone else. The Church says he can't get married again. His new wife is his bottle.... The Church doesn't care about that!"

"What do you believe then?" I asked, incredulous that he hadn't swallowed it all, as I had.

"All I know is, Jesus is a friend of mine! You don't need nothin' else." Michael put on his socks and boots. "Enough serious talk. Come on." Michael took me by the hand and pulled me up. "Let's go to the midnight show!"

"Really?" I hurriedly finished dressing. "I'm coming!" There was a new understanding between us. I understood in my heart that this night was our communion, the essence of marriage...not anything others could see on the outside. Not anything you could prove to your neighbor. I felt married to Michael. Even if no one validated our love, that night could never be lost. I knew I could be loved for the first time in my life.

The next two weeks were the happiest of my life. One morning Michael called me from the train depot in downtown St. Paul.

"Diana, listen. I can't talk long. I'm at the train depot. I've been drafted into the Army! I'm leaving right now."

"No, Michael. No! You told me you'd get a medical deferment. You can't leave me; you're all I have. Please, please don't leave. I'll die. I'll die!"

"Listen, the doctor never sent the letter he promised to send for my deferment. I think my dad talked him out of it. I don't know what happened...God, just please...I have to go, Sugar! I love you! Wait for me! I'll write to you on the train!"

I put the receiver down, laid my body on the kitchen

floor, and screamed hysterically, Why, why God? Please, make it not so! Please, God. I'll be good. I promise. I'll never sin again. Bring Michael back. Don't let them take him away! My fists pounded the floor. Please, please God! Make it not so! I love him! I love him! Please, please don't punish me this way! I cried for half an hour. When the sobbing subsided I thought, I could die now. What was there to live for? Had he known before the weekend? Had he set me up? Was it because I wasn't a virgin that he left? His father had never accepted that I was in the hospital. Maybe he'd talked Michael into going in the army when I was gone.

Devastated, I never went back to my job. I hid in the house ruminating. I convinced myself Michael had never loved me. How could anyone love me?

I received a letter from him three weeks later. He wrote and told me that he was going to Vietnam. He was afraid he might never come back. He wrote that he loved me and wanted me to wait for him. But I had convinced myself that he was lying. Everything had changed so fast.

I ran to the mailbox every day and bought the hit records *Mr. Postman* and *Soldier Boy* like thousands of other girls. We were the forgotten casualties of war.

On weekends I went over the state border to Wisconsin to dance with my sister and a group of girlfriends. They had a lower legal drinking age there. We all shared a motel room, sleeping on roll out cots and in sleeping bags on the floor.

I drowned my troubles in beer. The more I missed Michael, the more I danced and drank. We danced at a reno-vated barn in the country called "The Hoot." They had great bands and a huge dance floor. It was so far out in the country, the locals thought we were "city girls." They waited on week-ends for the "St. Paul Girls" to show up.

(Three of my friends are still married to the men they met in Wisconsin.)

One Spring weekend in a burst of energy, I cleaned my dad's house until it was spic and span. I even cleaned my room and packed a bag full of clothes to give to the Salvation Army.

That weekend my sister and I went to "The Hoot" alone. I
drank from 7:00 P.M. to midnight, drowning my sorrow in beer
and Bloody Marys trying to get drunk.

Back at the motel when I went into the bathroom to
change into my nightgown, I took the bottle of fifty-five
Thorazine tablets out of the zippered compartment of my
suitcase. I knew exactly how many there were. I'd been saving
them. (It was the bottle I'd received at the nursing home.) I
swallowed them, two at a time, choking and gagging on cup-
fuls of water getting them down. (Alcohol triples the effect of
tranquilizers like Thorazine.)

When I came out of the bathroom, I scribbled a short
note on a scrap of paper:

"Tell Michael I love him," and put it under my purse.

Still wearing my makeup and false eyelashes, I got into
bed. I cannot say how long I was there when I started to feel
drowsy. Suddenly I was aware of my twin sister getting into
bed next to me. I thought then how she would wake up to find
my dead body in the morning. Feeling guilty I leaned over and
told her about the overdose. "I took the pills. I took the pills.
I'm sorry. I have to go now!"

When she finally understood what I was saying, she ran
to get a friend we knew in the neighboring motel cabin. The
next thing I remember is being propped up by my arms, being
put in my sister's car, and being transported to the hospital. I
blacked out and woke up on a gurney being wheeled into an
emergency operating room. I remember saying, "Now will you
help me? Will you help me now?"

CHAPTER 10

"Light My Fire"

Six weeks later I found myself in the kitchen at home.

Dad was standing next to the sink drinking a glass of milk. I said to him, "Now you are all ready for prenatal care."

Something in my head snapped—I stood there, shocked. Why had I said such a bizarre thing to my father? I walked out of the kitchen into the living room, over to my father's desk and looked at the calendar. I'd lost six weeks. How had I survived? Where was I those six weeks?

My sister told me they had pumped my stomach at the hospital for over three hours.

She had called our parents' home that night, but the phone was downstairs and no one answered until the next afternoon. The doctor had informed Donna that my vital signs were not good and I would not live through the day. He explained that it was for the best because I would have permanent brain damage and have to be institutionalized if I survived.

I only had one memory of being at the hospital. I was in a small room by myself wearing a skimpy hospital gown. I remember pulling the sides together in back to keep my butt from showing. I stood at the window and waved down at Michael, whom I saw as clear as day standing in the grass waving up at me and smiling.

I was told it was an hallucination caused by the psychotropic drug as the effects left my body. Michael was in boot camp in Texas. I believed Michael's spirit had visited me. My sister told me I'd wandered around the house for six weeks acting like a two-year-old, moving objects from room to room.

I felt that my mother was angry with me, either because I was more disturbed than she and took attention away from my father, or because I had sinned against the Catholic Church by trying to take my own life. It was a sin worse than rape.

If I had continued hallucinating I'd have been put away forever. But, once again medical science had been wrong—I was alive and back to abnormal. No one suggested counseling and I wanted no part of it, anyway.

I was very weak and unable to make decisions for the next three weeks. I was still very thin and my hair was still very short but back to its natural color, a sandy brown. I could not make decisions for the next several weeks. My sister invited me to her company picnic in an effort to get me out of the house. It was a sunny July day. I wore navy blue pants with a white blouse and a striped navy and white summer blazer. Before the suicide attempt I had bought a hairpiece of long straight hair that exactly matched the color of my own hair. I wore it to the picnic.

My sister and I played games, ate popcorn, fries, and corn dogs, and listened to the bands performing in the pavilion. When night came, the outside lights illuminated tents and concession stands. Donna danced with a male friend from work. I watched from the side. A very big, handsome man with brown curly hair and brown eyes introduced himself to me. He was over six-foot-two and resembled James Garner. He appeared to be in his mid-twenties and told me he was with Ken, Donna's dance partner.

He sat down on the bench across from me and started telling me about himself. He was a foreman at a factory that manufactured appliances. He was articulate and charismatic and he impressed me with his confidence.

When I stood to dance with him, my hands got lost in his huge palms. We danced through the next four songs.

"Thanks, Hercules!" I said when the band stopped playing. Ken and Donna and Robert and I danced and talked together until the band packed up their instruments for the night.

Robert gave me a ride home in his white convertible and walked me up to the front door.

"I have a boyfriend in the service," I said.

"We can be friends!" He smiled. I wondered if he'd have asked for my phone number if he'd known the truth. I'd only gone to the picnic to forget about my suicide attempt. It seemed everyone else had already forgotten about it.

I gave Robert my phone number. "Nice meeting you," I said as he walked down the sidewalk to his car. He was so tall he made me feel petite.

I was glad I had gone out. I felt more alive, as though I were back in life again, but I was more unhappy than before the suicide attempt. No one had told me they wanted me to live. No one had asked me not to try it again. No one had asked me "Why" I was still depressed. Where could I go for help?

I was no longer Catholic and had no church. I would not go to a counselor only to be labeled and drugged. I had to find out what I believed in. Where had my soul been those weeks I had lost track of? I knew that God was not merciless and petty, as the Catholic Church had taught me. But who was God? Who was I? Why had God brought me out of the dark?

I can't prove it, but I know I "died" and was given a choice to return. I believe it was to share this book.

To my surprise, Robert did call back. We started to date. I was reluctant because I still loved Michael, but I justified it because I had convinced myself Michael had chosen to leave me because I was not a virgin.

Robert knew what a young girl wanted to hear. He told me I was beautiful when I felt I wasn't. He brought me gifts and made me feel like I was special. He had the storybook behavior of a prince. Even my mom was impressed. She told me it would be a "whirlwind courtship." I attended his softball games all summer, sitting on a lawn chair, rooting for the team along with his dad.

He spent money like water. One night he took me into
Wisconsin to a fancy restaurant. He ordered a seven-course
meal, complete with a bottle of wine for our table, lobster tail,
dessert, and after dinner, a fine liqueur. I was intrigued and
infatuated. Forgetting everything, I became absorbed in a
fantasy with this charming, older man.

The day after this elaborate dinner I wrote Robert a
poem. After I mailed it, I panicked, feeling certain that it would
frighten him away. I didn't hear from him for two days.

On the third day a delivery man arrived at the door with
a large box of fresh flowers. I signed for them and started up
the steps to my mom's room. I was sure they were for my
mother. I must have forgotten her birthday or something. As I
got upstairs I saw the card on the box. It read, "Diana, let these
speak for me until I can find the right words!" Signed, Robert.
Inside were a dozen, long-stemmed red roses. I was hooked.

He was everything I'd been taught a man should be: tall,
dark, handsome, generous, outgoing, athletic, and educated. He
was even Catholic. He had a good job and a beautiful family.
He was twenty-six and had a great sense of humor. Hercules,
as I called him, took me to places I'd never seen before. He
liked to surprise me.

One night we went to a downtown Minneapolis bar on
Hennepin Avenue called the Gay Nineties. (I didn't know the
meaning of gay yet.) The place was packed. People were lined
up outside waiting to get in, curious to see the show. There was
standing room only inside. Hercules waved down the bar
manager, calling him by name, and giving him a big tip. We
were shown to a reserved table right in front of the stage.

After a few drinks (no one questioned my age when I
was with Herc) the lights were dimmed and the stage show
began. The emcee, a buxom blonde named Lee, did a hilarious
comic routine. She looked familiar, but I couldn't figure out
where I'd seen her before.

Next, a half-dozen tall dancers came on stage in
skimpy, sequined outfits waving feathery fans in the air. After
a well-choreographed show the girls pranced off in their four-

inch high heels and Lee announced the star of the show, that Cuban bombshell, Shalimar! The crowd clapped and cheered, shouting Shalimar's name.

I watched in amazement as the black-haired, long-legged beauty appeared on stage, seductively draped in white fur. She sauntered across the floor and did a slow, sensual striptease. Her breasts appeared strangely round and hard, like giant muskmelons. When she had nothing on but her nylons and G-string I noticed she had no hips and her Adam's apple was unusually large. She looked familiar.

The hospital! That's where I'd seen both Lee and Shalimar before! It was too loud in the bar to talk. When Robert and I went out for coffee afterwards I told him that I'd seen Shalimar and Lee before.

"Where?" he asked.

"In the hospital!" I said.

"When you were a nurse's aide?" He asked.

"No....I may as well tell you," I fumbled getting my gloves off. "I had kind of a breakdown. When I was in the psych ward Lee and Shalimar were there, too."

"Gee, maybe I saw you there. I visited Shalimar in the hospital before the operation." Robert poured coffee from a thermal pot into both our cups.

"What operation?" I asked.

"Don't you know," he laughed. "Shalimar and Lee are transsexuals. They had sex-change operations from male to female!"

"You're kidding me!" I couldn't quite fathom it. "But why were they in the psych ward?"

"To have psychological tests to be sure they could adjust to the change." Robert explained to me that Minnesota was known worldwide as one of the few places where trans-sexual operations were performed.

He was surprised I hadn't known because the newspapers were exploiting the controversial surgery, creating an audience of curiosity seekers for Lee and Shalimar. Before a sex change was performed the candidate had to undergo exten-

sive testing in the hospital and live as the opposite sex for a
year before surgery. The operation was so complex it could not
be reversed. Hormone injections were required after surgery.
Robert told me that Lee's breasts were his/her own. They'd
grown after taking female hormones. Shalimar's on the other
hand, were implants.

I was impressed that Robert could be so matter-of-fact
about such an unusual thing. He had made no judgment about
it. They were two people he knew. He didn't idolize nor condemn them.

"Why were you depressed?" Robert asked.

"I don't know. They never really helped me figure it
out. Part of it was because my mom's been sick for so long. I
felt guilty living when she was dying."

"My dad is sick, too," Robert confessed. "He's got
leukemia."

"But he's so active! He's still working!" His father
seemed so healthy.

"It's in remission, but it could get worse at any time!"

We talked for hours that night about parents and illness
and how intolerant society was of people's differences. Robert
was able to joke about it. I still thought it was a depressing
world to be in and it didn't look as if it were going to change to
me.

That night when I was trying to sleep I wondered why
God would put a soul into the wrong body in the first place.
The religious beliefs I'd had since birth came into question
again with a vengeance. Hadn't Jesus said to love everyone, to
see Christ in all people? Of course, I couldn't understand what
kind of feelings could drive people to take such drastic mea-
sures as altering their bodies. But maybe they had been in the
same vulnerable place I had been in. I decided I shouldn't judge
them. I felt relieved with my decision.

Although I had left the institution of the Church, no
matter what people believed about me, I never stopped believ-

ing in God. Even in my suicide attempts I had been attempting to leave the world of suffering I'd been taught was life, in order to find a better place. After being raped, the Church had excluded me by its sexist dogma and narrow interpretation of mercy. The only sin worse than losing one's virginity, for a woman, was a suicide attempt. The Church had no room for people like me or Lee or Shalimar.

Some of my Catholic friends prayed for my soul because I was a "fallen Catholic," and doomed to burn in hell. Many people assumed (and still assume) that if you did not belong to an institutionalized religion, you were an atheist. But I knew so many people who only attended church for social and political reasons. I knew many churchgoers who had no spiritual beliefs and no love for anyone outside their small circle of family and friends.

I still questioned why God had saved me. What was it God wanted me to do with my life?

One night in September, after watching Robert play football, I went out with his team to celebrate. We went to Hafner's where his mom bowled. He ordered me a Harvey Wallbanger, a "suicide" drink that included several shots of hard liquor. Still not an experienced drinker, I had a reputation for getting high just by sniffing the cork. After one Harvey I was a pile of silly putty. After the celebration ended Hercules drove me to Duluth Playground, a secluded park near his house.

It was about 2:00 A.M. We were singing and giggling as we got out of the car. We ended up far away from the road under an oak tree. As he lowered me to the earth he told me he loved me. Robert had knowledge of a woman's body that I'd never been warned about. He touched places that no one had touched before. I was consumed with the urgency to unite with Robert. After that night the song "Light My Fire" was our song.

We were a couple. We talked every night. He still

bought me expensive dinners and gifts. For my birthday he gave me a pink brocade music box that played "Strangers in the Night."

I had not received a letter from Michael since the letter he'd written on the train. It had been nearly four months. Sometimes I missed him, but I was still denying the anger I felt because I believed he had abandoned me without a commitment. If he had proposed to me I never would have gone to that company picnic. I might never have taken the overdose had I known that anger was human and not a sin. Anger is a normal feeling when you are afraid of losing someone.

I'd been carefully taught to deny anger, but I now know that anger turned inward equals suicide. How many victims of religion's hypocrisy are buried in the earth right now? The Church wanted me delivered to hell, but God had other plans for me.

It was October, the day after I attended the University of Minnesota Homecoming Dance with Hercules, that I found out for sure—I was pregnant.

CHAPTER 11

"Love Child"

Robert picked me up from the clinic the day I found out I was pregnant. When I told him, he would not remove his sunglasses. He frowned and drove silently through the streets, taking me directly home. As he opened the car door for me and waited for me to get out, he said: "I need time to think."

I watched as he got in the driver's seat and took off, squealing the tires as he tore away. This was not the way Prince Charming would have handled it.

Even though Robert had gone away to think about it I felt that my life mattered suddenly. I wanted to give birth to this baby, with or without him. But I knew I was emotionally only a child myself and feared I could not handle motherhood, especially without a husband.

I made arrangements with the welfare department to release my baby for adoption after it was born.

I was not going to tell my parents until I could move into the unwed mothers' home, where I'd planned to stay until the birth. But that plan was changed when Robert sent my father a letter at his office telling him I was pregnant. In the letter he denied that he was the father and accused Michael of getting me pregnant before he went in the service.

Dad showed me the letter when he got home that day. He handled it pretty calmly. I told him that I had already made arrangements to go away and give the baby up for adoption.

But I didn't want Mom to know until I left for the home.

I wrote Robert a letter and told him what my plans were and how badly the letter he'd sent my dad had hurt me. I had no doubt the baby was his and tests could easily prove that. I didn't want his sympathy or money. If he didn't love me, it was best that I give our baby up. Maybe in some way I could make up for attempting suicide by bringing this baby into the world. Maybe that was why I'd been saved.

I had been so sure Robert had been sincere. He was the prince who did everything I'd been taught a "good man should." He'd included me in his life, introduced me to his family, spent lots of money on me, told me he loved me.

Because I was "honest to a fault," I had believed everyone was as honest as I was. How could I trust my own perceptions any longer? Of course, inside I felt I deserved to be abused because of my sinfulness. I had been taught we were alive to suffer. I felt guilty when I was happy! I couldn't understand fully how those beliefs, which I took literally had created the circumstances I drew to me, until I learned that I could change the beliefs I'd been taught. I had many more tests to take before I would learn the truth.

I was more afraid of how my mother would react to the news that I was not a virgin than I was of going away or delivering a baby. Two months earlier I'd overheard her talking to Robert while I was getting dressed. She had told him that her daughters were virgins. I was embarrassed! She'd been oblivious to everything that had gone on in my life for years. My mother was living in a fantasy world.

By the time Robert had been gone for three weeks, the old depression returned. I had already gained back all of the weight I'd lost in the hospital and more. Mom was starting to make remarks that I'd better watch my weight or I'd lose Robert. She hadn't yet realized he was gone. Secretly, I believed he'd have a change of heart and come back to me.

About six weeks later in the evening, I received a phone call. Robert had another person call and ask for me.

"It's for you." My dad handed me the receiver.

There was muffled talking and then Robert came to the phone.

"Diana, this is Robert. Please don't hang up on me. I want to help you through this."

Dad was watching me. I couldn't say anything.

"Meet me at the playground tonight—nine o'clock."

Before I had decided whether to meet him or not, Dad reached over and took the phone out of my hands.

"I know who this is. You're not welcome in this house. Don't call here again!" He hung up the phone.

I was stunned that Dad stood up for me and angry that he stopped me from seeing Robert.

"Thanks a lot!" I said and ran up to my room and slammed the door. The one image that kept returning to my mind had nothing to do with Robert. Something about the urgency in Robert's voice when he had asked me to meet him reminded me of Steve. Cold snow flurries filled the air as they had that night, reminding me of Steve's lie that his grandmother had died—the oil-stained garage floor—the rape. I remembered the letter Robert had written to my father. Was he so different from Steve? Were all men selfish cowards?

I had taken responsibility for the pregnancy. I was going to bring a baby into the world. That was all that mattered. For once I heard the soft inner warning whispering "Don't go." I was sick. I put my head under the pillow to muffle the tears, afraid I would wake my mother and I cried myself to sleep.

In the next few weeks I fought with myself. Part of me wanted to see Robert, wanted to be held, wanted any support I could get during the pregnancy. My sister convinced me that Robert was not sincere. There were rumors that he'd been seeing other women while he was seeing me. I didn't want to believe that. He'd been so attentive and so generous. How could he find time or afford to see anyone else? If that were true, why had he called me back at all?

Then I received a letter from Michael. In the letter he told me about boot camp and the army and small talk. He said he loved me. It was obvious he thought everything was the same as it had been before he'd left. I was heartsick. I wrote him back and told him how I had believed he didn't love me anymore because I wasn't a virgin and because I'd been hospitalized. I told him about the suicide attempt, about dating Robert, and about the pregnancy. I was sorry for everything. I'd been stupid. I would always love him. I thanked him for showing me what true love was. I believed again that he really never had stopped loving me. But I couldn't undo what I had done.

Robert didn't call back. By the first of December everything was set up for me to go to the unwed mothers' home. That day Mom was out of her bedroom. She was in a Dexedrine spin, in a cleaning frenzy. I was sitting on the sofa when she vacuumed over my feet.

When I got up she shut off the vacuum and told me, "You look like two kids fighting under a blanket from the back. You'd better lose weight!"

The words fell off my tongue.

"I'm pregnant."

Hysterically, she screamed, "My God, My God! No. No! How could you? What kind of a tramp are you?" She retreated quickly to her bedroom.

She refused to open the door, even for my father, and refused to eat. My dad stood vigil at the door for four days, begging her to let him in. No one could be sure what drugs she was taking. She spent hours sobbing, moaning, and chanting. But it was worse when she was quiet. We didn't know if she had overdosed or not.

There was an undeclared war at home. A cold war and I was the enemy. What had made my mother so frightened? It was ironic that my mom, who was so religious, could not forgive me. It was something I would observe again and again—that the most outwardly religious were often the most judgmental and least forgiving. If I could just learn to stop reacting to her!

The morning of December sixth I woke up sweating profusely. There was blood on the sheet. I was scared. As I got up and rolled the sheets off the bed, a pain shot through my groin. I slowly put on a clean nightgown and took a set of clean sheets out of the hall linen closet.

I smoothed the sheets over the bed without tucking them in and laid down again. I was in a daze and went in and out of sleep. At about 9:00 A.M. the contractions started. The pain was excruciating. I held tightly to the base of the head-board, gritted my teeth, and prayed for the pain to end. When I went to the bathroom I passed several large blood clots. By noon the clean sheets were wringing wet from perspiration. I was having a miscarriage. The blood was running out of me.

By the time Dad got home from work I was screaming with pain. I tried to find a comfortable position, but nothing helped. I was losing my mind. I was only four months along. How could it hurt so much?

Without warning Mom unlocked her bedroom door and came out from hiding.

"I'm calling an ambulance!" Dad went into the bedroom and walked to the phone.

"No, you're not!" Mother screamed. "Put that phone down! No ambulance! The neighbors will find out she's preg-nant!"

Dad put the phone down, left the dark bedroom, and came over to me.

"Let's go. I'll take you to the hospital myself."

Mother retreated to the bedroom, slammed the door, and locked it behind her.

"I need my robe." I bent over, holding my abdomen.

Dad retrieved my robe from the closet and helped me down the stairs, through the door, and down the front steps to the car. I laid down in the back seat for the ride to the hospital.

By the time I got to the emergency room the contrac-tions were coming close together. I was having contractions while the doctor examined me on a cart in the emergency room.

The examining physician lectured to an intern about miscarriage while I grabbed the side of the cart, preparing for another contraction.

"It looks like a placenta previa miscarriage. Very dangerous. It causes effusive hemorrhaging!"

This was a bad dream. I was a human textbook.

"Why didn't you get here sooner?" The doctor asked.

I couldn't answer. I was faint. My eyes were rolling back in my head.

When I became alert again an admission clerk came over to me with a clipboard and asked me for billing information. The contractions were coming non-stop. When she had my signature on the dotted line I was taken to a private room and given a hypo for the pain. Exhausted, I fell asleep.

When I woke up the pain was gone. I sat up and moved to the side of the bed. Too weak to get to the bathroom I took a bedpan off the dressing table, closed the curtains around my bed, lifted myself on, and passed several blood clots.

When I got off, floating in the bedpan was a small fetus. It was white and only as big as my thumb. It seemed too small to have survived four months. It must have stopped developing earlier. I felt numb and empty inside. I rang for the nurse.

When she came in I showed her my baby. She frowned, mumbled that it was "for the best," and carried the bedpan into the bathroom. With the door still open she flushed the fetus down the toilet, right in front of me.

She could have at least taken it into another room. I remembered my mom telling me how she had baptized fetuses when she worked as a nurse in delivery. She believed the baby had to be baptized to go to heaven or else the soul would go to limbo until it received enough grace to go to heaven.

I didn't believe it. How could God punish an innocent soul? Was the soul still in the fetus if it died earlier in the womb? If we were souls then God had the power to give that soul life in another body. It could be born to someone else, in another fetus. How did the Church know how it worked? I would never send an innocent soul to limbo or hell. There was no way that God could have less love and forgiveness than I did. No scripture would convince me otherwise. Faith was beginning to stir again in my life. The living Spirit, not the caricature the Church had invented to keep us in line and in debt for its absolution.

My sister and Dad visited me that night. He told me that Mom had been admitted to the hospital. He couldn't stay long because he had to visit her. I didn't know what was wrong. He told me that only he could see her.

The next day I had a D&C to scrape my uterus. I was given a hypo for pain, but I was awake for the whole thing. I had not been prepared to see the doctor training three interns at the other end of the operating room table. There I was with my legs spread like a wish-bone, with four men observing the operation. I felt like a lab animal.

After surgery, the doctor said matter-of-factly, "No intercourse for at least a week, now," and grinned. What an ass he was. He didn't know me.

By the time I was back home, Mom was already out of the hospital and back in seclusion in her bedroom. She still wouldn't talk to me. I decided it was time for me to move out of the house.

Just before Christmas I received a letter from Michael. He had written that he still loved me. And he was going to Vietnam in April.

CHAPTER 12

"Where's The Playground, Susie?"

It was in November of 1968 when I applied for an assembly job at a factory downtown where they packaged hair care products. I was thrilled when I got the job.

Advertised in the newspaper was a room for rent located downtown in an old mansion on the corner of Exchange and Cedar. I made an appointment with the caretaker to see the room. It would be perfect. It was within walking distance to work.

When I got off the bus and walked down Cedar I looked for the boarding house called Central Manor, now the Exchange Building. As the corner building caught my eye, I realized it was the same place where I had once visited Sister Mary Patrick. She was the nun who had chosen me to lead the May procession when I was in fourth grade at Blessed Sacrament. Central Manor had once been a convent.

The caretaker explained the building was one of the oldest in St. Paul. It had originally been a music conservatory. As she showed me around I was surprised how little had changed since the nuns had been there.

Large old religious paintings still hung in the hallways. The lounge where the Sisters had greeted visitors still had the same antique furniture, light green carpeting, and ceramic tile fireplace. High ceilings and dark oak woodwork gave the place a heavy, sullen feeling. As I followed the caretaker through the corridors to my room, a pungent, musty odor filled the air, making me feel as if I were going back in time.

As we walked down the last corridor I noticed that three steps led up to a higher floor at the end of the hallway. At the top of the steps was Room 7. The woman unlocked the door and showed me into the room. The only window was made of leaded stained glass and depicted priests preparing the sacrament of the Holy Eucharist, holding the host to heaven. The outside light from the alley filtered softly through the exquisite colors, drawing me in. This was no ordinary room.

There was an indefinable presence there.

The room was furnished with a small bed and dresser and a small closet for storage. I wondered if this had been the room where Sister Mary Patrick had stayed.

The caretaker showed me through the rest of the manor. There were three large bathrooms with stalls similar to the ones we had in parochial school. One of the lavatories had several old porcelain bathtubs. I could imagine Sister carrying her towel down the hall to the lavatory where she modestly bathed behind the stall door.

Laundry facilities and a communal kitchen were on the basement level. A senior citizen high-rise had been built right next to Central Manor. Residents were allowed to purchase hot meals there three times a day. It had everything I needed!

"I'll take it!"

Dad moved me in that weekend.

That first night when I turned out the lights it was very dark in the small, narrow room. I felt as though someone were there with me. It wasn't a frightening presence I felt, but more of a maternal feeling that enveloped me. Just before falling asleep I saw flickering lights in the corner of the room. They must have been some kind of shadow from a car passing through the alley, although I hadn't heard anything outside.

The assembly job went well. I had good hand dexterity. Every day new employees were let go for not meeting quota, but I had passed the first line, folding cartons and packing bottles of permanent wave.

The long-timers warned me about the last line we'd be tested on where the cans of hair spray came down the belt really fast. The assemblers had to attach a circular cardboard band around the hair spray can that held a free comb. The cardboard sleeve fit so tightly around the can that it was difficult to get it on without tearing it. If a worker wasn't fast enough, the cans would pile up and the entire line would have to be shut down. If that happened, the person would be out of a job. If a worker made it through the probation period, he or she would be protected by the union. I would worry about that when I got there.

One Saturday morning a woman knocked on my door and said I had a call. The only phone I could use was out in the hallway. It was Dad. He told me he'd had a heart attack and was being hospitalized for testing. He'd had a pain in his shoulder and arm ever since he'd helped me move out.

Tests showed that he had blocked arteries and high cholesterol. They immediately put him on a strict regimen of diet and exercise. Eventually he would require heart surgery. I felt guilty, but I wasn't moving back home.

Terry, the youngest of my three brothers, moved home to be with Mom while Dad was hospitalized.

It was December. After the holidays, Terry and another brother Peter left for India to study Transcendental Meditation.

What impressed me most was that once you learned TM, you could use it on your own. You did not need to join the "organization," worship a master, change your religion, diet, or friends.

The theory was simple: Life creates stress—stress causes emotional and physical imbalance and suffering. You could release the stress daily through meditation before it manifested into mental and physical illness.

It had been scientifically proven that TM slowed the

metabolism down lower than in deep sleep, thus releasing deep stress from the central nervous system.

My brothers promised to teach me how to meditate when they came home from India.

Back at Central Manor, I loved my new-found independence, having my own space and my own cash. Sometimes I thought about Robert and fantasized that he was the man I believed he was when I met him—that he'd miss me and come back to me. I was still emotionally an eleven-year-old in a nineteen-year-old body.

On February eighth I stopped in a local cafe for breakfast. Several customers were sitting at the counter having a heated discussion about the murder of a sixteen-year-old girl on the Lower East Side. I asked the waitress what they were talking about. I had no radio or television in my room.

She handed me the morning newspaper. Susan Merek had been brutally murdered. Her nude body had been found on a playground with her hands taped behind her. She'd been strangled and run over by a car. The most heinous aspect of the murder was that the killer had forced a tire iron into the girl's vagina. Everyone in the cafe agreed that the murderer deserved castration and execution. The police had a suspect, but no one had been apprehended.

The jukebox in the cafe was playing current hit records. A chill went down my spine when I heard the lyrics of the next song..."Where's the playground, Susie?"

I finished my breakfast and left. I didn't want to hear any more about the dangers of young girls being in the streets. It was dark in the morning when I walked to work downtown. I felt safer in the winter when I was covered with a coat. It was below zero and bitterly cold.

I felt independent and best of all—not a burden to anyone. That was what mattered. I had no other choice. I was not going to go home and watch my mother rot in that room. If I were murdered I'd go to heaven as a martyr anyway and everyone would be happy. That was the least of my worries. I had no control over murderers. I had no control over my mother's illness. I tried to concentrate on what I could control in order to survive.

One evening as I was frying a hamburger in the kitchen, a resident came in to fix herself supper. Her name was Ellen. Her hair was short and she was very large. We shared stories of how we had ended up living at Central Manor. She held a clerical job downtown and had moved to St. Paul from a small town up north. I told her I had once visited a nun at Central Manor when it was a convent. It was then the subject turned to religion.

Ellen told me she was a Spiritualist, a Christian who believed that we were all Spirit and had been given a body as a vehicle for learning. She told me the minister of her church was a woman, a psychic medium who communicated with spirits who had passed over into the spiritual realm.

She believed there were spiritual guides and entities who could help us on this plane. This was not unlike the Catholic belief in praying to angels and saints. This felt true for me. It did not conflict with Jesus' teaching of everlasting life.

The main difference was that the Spiritualists believed in using the free will, intelligence, and intuition God had given them in order to find their own unique path. They had no false gods wearing costumes who set themselves above them as authorities. And they believed in healing more than in hell.

I invited Ellen to come to my room and visit with me. I thought there was a presence in my room and I wondered if she could feel it, too. She told me she could perform a séance. That night she came to my room and brought a ouija board and a candle.

I told Ellen that I had been taught that the ouija board was the devil. She said she always prayed for protection before communicating with the other side and that we would be safe from any lower entities coming through. I shut off the lights. Ellen lit the candle and we waited.

Sister Lucy, before leaving the convent.

My family in the earlier years.

At age five my twin
sister Donna and I at
my aunt's cabin.

My first date with
my first love, Michael.

Kenny (my son at age 12) and I, bonded by the struggle for survival.

Bill, my husband, and Kenny shortly after we met in 1981.

I finally meet Steve Allen, September 15, 1990.

Sharing my happiness and peace with Bill.

CHAPTER 13

"Black Magic Woman"

Ellen took two pillows off the bed and threw them on the floor. "We'll sit on these," she said. "When the flame of the candle turns in a circular motion, an entity is present."

Ellen adjusted the pillow under her large body. I settled down, folded my legs, and anxiously waited for the séance to begin.

After twenty long minutes the candle flame slowly began to twirl clockwise.

"Stay still!" Ellen opened her hands and lifted them in the air. "There is a benevolent spirit present." Ellen's voice trembled.

I stopped myself from clearing my throat, afraid to move.

"I see a woman in a black gown. No, no, it's a habit. Yes, it's the spirit of a nun! She's smiling." Ellen looked towards the stained glass window.

"She says she lived here in the convent." Ellen put her hands up to her face. Her expression looked sad.

"She says she died here in the chapel during Mass." Ellen tilted her head as if to hear better.

I didn't hear the voice Ellen heard, but I felt an unmistakable feeling of someone's presence—the same feeling I had when I first saw the room.

Ellen shut her eyes and started to rock back and forth on the pillow.

"The connection is weak. I'm going to meditate for a few minutes here and try again."

I waited with my eyes open, hoping I would get a glimpse of the nun. I thought about how my spiritual feelings had been aroused since I had moved into Central Manor. I had even half-heartedly resumed attending Mass at the Catholic Church across the street. I also had purchased several religious paintings at an antique store to hang in my room. But I still could not reconcile the negative dogma of the Church with the truth I knew. I had asked God for guidance and for someone to share my new positive belief in God with. That's when I had met Ellen.

Spiritualism appealed to me. Because we are spirit we have everlasting life, as Christ promised. It understood the main reason Jesus had come—to prove that we never die.

Smoke from the candle brought me out of my reverie. The flame had gone out.

Ellen opened her eyes, looking distressed.

"I know this spirit had a message for you." She shrugged her shoulders. "I'm sorry. I just couldn't get it."

Ellen got up and took her ouija board out of the box.

"I'm going to try this—maybe I can get her back." Ellen sat back down on the pillow, braced her back against the bed and placed the board on her knees. She prayed out loud:

"Light of God
Surround us.
Nothing but good
shall come to us.
Nothing but good
shall go from us."

Ellen set the tear-shaped plastic pointer at the bottom center of the board and placed her fingers lightly on the end of the object.

"What should I do?" I whispered.

"Nothing. Usually it takes two people, but it works by itself with me." She went on to explain, "This thing will answer questions by spelling; it points to the letters of the alphabet. It can answer in numbers or point to the words Yes and No at the corners of the board."

"It's already moving!" Ellen gasped.

The pointer appeared to pull Ellen's hands around the board. It moved in a haphazard pattern, too quick and jerky to spell discernible words.

Ellen sighed heavily and took her hands off the pointer.

We watched, spellbound, as the pointer continued to move by itself. We hoped to decipher any message that might come through.

After two or three minutes watching the object scramble back and forth across the board without making sense, I was terrified.

"Stop it. Stop it, Ellen! Please, stop it!"

Ellen vigorously shook her head and raised the palm of her hand to me. "Just a few more minutes. I'm getting something here."

I waited, praying silently for the séance to end. I had to live in that room. Ellen didn't.

After about five more minutes of erratic movement the pointer slid over the board and flew off onto the floor.

Ellen was deep in thought. The color had drained from her face. "It's over," she said.

"What did it say?" I asked. "Did you get anything?"

She hesitated, as if deciding what to tell me and what to withhold.

"I....I got a message....but it's only words....and I don't know what it means."

"Tell me. Tell me." I pulled on the sleeve of Ellen's blouse.

"All right! All I could get was, 'Ski, Ski....Kill...Kill!' Does that make any sense to you?"

"No." I stood up, stretched, turned on the light, and sat down on my bed. "I don't get it."

"Maybe you're going to get killed in a ski accident?" Ellen speculated.

"No, no....I don't even ski. And I'm certainly not going

to learn, if that's what it meant."

"I guess that's not it." Ellen smiled.

We both heaved a sigh of relief. We were being silly. It probably didn't mean anything.

Ellen picked up her candle and ouija board.

"You're not leaving are you?" I stood up.

"I have to. My dad's picking me up after work, at midnight. He works the night shift. I'm going home for the weekend." Ellen opened the door. "Don't worry. Your spirit is a friend! She won't hurt you. She'll protect you!"

"Oh, great!" I rolled my eyes. "Just great!"

"But, I still feel like she was trying to warn you about something outside of Central Manor. So be careful!" Ellen stepped out into the hallway.

"And whatever you do....don't go skiing!" She laughed a deep belly laugh.

"Very funny, Ellen. Very funny." I stood at the door. "Please call me when you get back, okay?"

"Sure." Ellen waved as she walked down the three steps. "Don't worry. I'll be praying for you!"

"Thanks." I stood by the door until she was out of sight, afraid to go back into the room. God knows what she had stirred up in there. She was so calm about it. It was all new to me.

I prayed the Our Father fifty times in a row and started a string of Hail Marys. It didn't help. I was too frightened to stay alone in the room, so I put on my coat and gloves, left the Manor, and walked to an all-night diner located at St. Peter and Ninth. Mickey's Diner was a renovated streetcar and a well-known eatery in St. Paul, located across from the bus depot. It was a stopover for travelers and transients.

I ordered coffee and toast, wondering how I would be able to hang out there until dawn without being kicked out. I wished I had a book or even some paper or a pen with me to write. But I'd left in a hurry, not even sure where I was going. I'd decided to see the priest across the street from the Manor about doing an exorcism.

Looking out the window I noticed there was a newspaper box outside at the curb. I told the waitress that I was going to buy a paper, that I'd be right back. Again the front page headline was about the murder of the girl on the East Side. As I read the latest news in the search for a suspect, the next record of the jukebox in the corner of the cafe flipped down and began to play "...where's the playground, Susie?" A chill went down my spine.

I didn't want to think about death after just having witnessed a séance. Why would the spirit of a nun, who had devoted herself to God in life, not be with Jesus? Why would a spirit hang around a dusty old building? And now this senseless murder of a sixteen-year-old and the eerie lyrics of a record that had been released before her death.

There were two men sitting at the counter eating. The cook was preparing food, and the waitress was filling the large coffee percolator with water. I put a quarter in the jukebox and chose three selections: "Love Child," "Mr. Postman," and "Walk On By."

One of the men at the counter came over and asked me if he could join me. Before I answered, he had carried his plate and coffee cup over and sat down across from me in the booth.

I felt sick inside. I didn't want to leave and risk him following me. I didn't want to go back to Room 7 and didn't want to talk to anyone just then. He seemed to sense my fear and told me to relax, that he was harmless.

We started out talking about the murder. His name was John. He had brown hair, blue eyes, and was tall and thin. He wore a khaki shirt, jeans, and a jean jacket. His face was tan and weary. He told me he was thirty-three, but he looked like he was about forty-five. To a twenty-year-old, thirty seemed ancient. He chain-smoked Camels as he told me his life story. I was a captive audience, not wanting to leave the diner until the dawn arrived.

John knew the cook and waitress. We could stay there for hours. John paid for my meal and an endless flow of coffee.

As a child John had lived with his mother, who was chronically ill with colitis and heavily sedated on a prescription drug called tincture of opiate, a derivative of opium. I could relate to that because of my own mother's medically-prescribed addiction. He had two brothers and two sisters. The family lived on welfare. When John was fourteen his mother had kicked his father out of the house and then reported to the police that his father was a deserter. In those days deserting your wife and children was punishable by imprisonment, so his father ran off and never returned.

John had pretty much scraped by, living in the streets. He'd learned to survive by petty thievery and worked his way up to picking locks and combination safes.

When he was eighteen he was caught forging payroll checks and was given a twenty-year prison sentence. In the forties and fifties, you received a double sentence if you had a prior felony. Due to good behavior he had been given a complete discharge after serving fifteen years incarceration in Stillwater Prison.

He had been out of prison less than a year.

John told me many horror stories about prison life. He wrote lyrics for country-western music. I was surprised that someone who had been locked up for so long was so sentimental.

By the time the sun came up that morning he had me convinced that we were soulmates.

CHAPTER 14

"You've Got to Change Your Evil Ways"

Instead of getting an exorcism I concentrated on work and tried not to think about the spirit in the room. It was a cold, cold February. I looked forward to Spring.

One evening, after supper, I received a phone call on the pay phone in the hallway.

"Diana, have you seen the newspaper?"

It was Shelly, my friend from high school.

"Not today. Why?"

"Robert's picture is on the front page!"

"You're kidding me. What for?"

"For the murder of Susan Merek. He's a prime suspect."

I didn't believe Shelly. It was probably her sadistic idea of a joke.

"I don't believe it. He was never violent with me."

"Honest, Diana. Cross my heart and hope to die! Go get a paper and see for yourself." Shelly sounded amused by the whole thing. She loved being the bearer of rotten news.

"I will. I'll call you later!" I hung up and ran to get my coat.

I rushed to a newspaper box to buy an evening paper. My heart pounded so fast I could feel the pulse in my forehead.

Before I had the paper out of the box I saw Robert's

picture on the front page. It was true. Robert had been picked up for the murder of Susan Merek. Her mutilated body had been found on Duluth Playground. "....Robert Petraszewski pleads innocent."

My head felt like it was going to explode. Duluth Playground was the playground where Robert and I had made love. He'd never been violent with me. He couldn't be a murderer! Sure he'd left me when I got pregnant, but lots of men do that.

What possible motive did he have? Robert was the All-American boy: charming, handsome, witty, educated, and employed. He played football, softball, and was on the bowling league. His family was close. His dad and mom were nice people. He came from a good Catholic family and had all the external qualities society emulated and encouraged young women to look for in a man.

Distraught and in denial, I went back to Room 7 and wrote a letter to Robert, in care of his attorney, whose name I had gotten from the newspaper. I told Robert about the miscarriage and explained that I had just heard about the murder. I wanted him to convince me he was innocent. The paper had said that the evidence against him was overwhelming.

Within five days I had received a letter from Robert. He wrote that he felt awful about what he'd done to me, that he still loved me. He told me that he was innocent but he couldn't tell me any more until the case came to trial.

His letter had only confused me more. The Robert I knew was not a killer. But what about the Robert that Susan Merek had known? Maybe he had a split personality? There was so much publicity about the murder that they moved the trial to another county in order to find an unbiased jury. Most people said they believed he was guilty.

I slept poorly that night and forgot to set the alarm clock. When I got up for work I was late. I had only three days of probation to go and I would be in the union. I hurriedly dressed and ran to work.

It was ten degrees below zero. As I ran, cold air was

forced into my lungs. By the time I got there, I was wheezing. After fifteen minutes on the hair spray line I had an asthma attack.

I took two ephedrine sulfate tablets and went to the nurse's office to rest until the pills took effect. During the hour that I rested, the nurse cross-examined me. I explained to her my history of allergies. When I recovered from the bronchial spasms I went back to work. But the nurse behaved strangely. I worked apprehensively for the rest of my shift.

When the whistle blew, signaling the shift's end, I was called into the office and told that "they" believed I had an allergic reaction to the chemicals used in the hair care products so "they" had to terminate my employment (conveniently before I could earn union wages).

I explained that the asthma had been a reaction to the cold air, but the personnel manager laughed in my face. "You're young. You can easily get a receptionist job!"

I left in a daze. I should never have run to work. It would have been better to be late. I'd still have a job. This couldn't be happening to me. All I wanted was to be independent. Now where would I go?

As I walked back to Central Manor, the words from the ouija board shouted in my head — "Ski, Ski. Kill, Kill!" Suddenly, I made the connection. Robert's last name was Petraszewski!

Had he killed Susan Merek? Had the spirit of a nun tried to protect me, to warn me not to see Robert? What would have happened if I'd met Robert the night Dad took the phone out of my hand? Would he have murdered me?

When I got back to Central Manor I went straight to Ellen's room, told her about being fired, and explained what I thought the message from the ouija board had meant.

"I didn't know you dated this guy!" Ellen motioned for me to sit down on her sofabed.

"I didn't just date him. I got pregnant. He left me and I had a miscarriage!"

"Oh, don't tell me that! My God, you are one lucky woman!"

"What do you mean?"

"Haven't you heard the rumors?"

"What rumors?"

"It's only hearsay, but people are saying he lured other girls to that playground. He is a suspect in the rape of a twelve-year-old girl there last summer."

My mind reeled. Had he gotten other girls pregnant also? What if he had gotten to me first? According to the paper he had lured Susan from a babysitting job. It was public knowledge that Robert had also dated the woman Susan babysat for. How many women had he been seeing when he dated me?

Why had God spared me from a fatal suicide attempt, from a dangerous miscarriage, and from a murder? Why hadn't God spared Susan Merek? Nothing made any sense. If Robert had brutally murdered a sixteen-year-old girl, how could I trust my own perceptions? I thought he was normal.

"I'm going to talk with the pastor at the Catholic Church across the street. I can't go back to my room, benevolent spirit or not!"

"Don't, Diana. Come to my church. You know, he's just going to blame you again. And tell you you're a sinner. You've been a victim long enough."

"I can't wait, Ellen. I need help now!"

"Well, talk to him, but that's all. I'll see if I can get ahold of my minister and get you an appointment."

"Thanks, thanks for being a friend. I don't know what's happening to me!" I gave Ellen a hug and left her room.

The housekeeper at the rectory answered the door and led me into the library to speak with the priest. The gray-haired father sat behind a large mahogany desk.

"How can I help you?" He stood and extended his hand to me.

I shook his hand and sat down in a large brocade chair across from him and started by telling the priest how I had visited the convent as a child.

His eyes lit up and he went into a lengthy history of the building, once owned by the Church.

"I said Mass in the convent chapel for years...."

He shared with me the story of Mother Francis Cabrini, a famous saint who had once stayed overnight in the convent.

"Why did the convent have a chapel of its own, with such a large church across the street?" I asked.

"Many of the retired nuns were elderly and infirm and not mobile enough to come to the Church."

"Where exactly was the chapel located?" I asked.

"Oh, let's see now. It's been renovated so many times since then." Father pointed out the window of his office toward Central Manor. "It was on the side of the building near the alley. In fact, I think the stained glass windows are still there."

I realized suddenly that the three steps leading to Room 7 had once led to the altar of the chapel. The altar had once been in the exact space of my room!

I recalled the flickering lights I'd "imagined" the first night I moved in and many nights after. They had resembled votive candles lit in offering of prayer and devotion, the kind I had lit in our church as a child, offering up prayers for my mother's healing.

The priest spoke kindly of his memories of the convent.

Trusting him, I told him the story of the rape, the pregnancy, and the miscarriage. Once I started talking I couldn't stop. He remained silent as I told him about my suicide attempt and my search for new faith. I was finally getting to the part about the murder and losing my job when he interrupted.

"Slow down. Where is your boyfriend now?" Father looked at me compassionately.

"Father, the worst part is that the murder suspect in the Susan Merek case—you know, in the papers?"

"Yes, what about him?"

"He's the man who got me pregnant. I don't know what to do. I need an exorcism. There's a spirit in my room. It tried to warn me about the murder. I don't understand why he didn't kill me." I rambled on, "Please help me."

"What do you mean, spirit?" the priest asked.

"It's the spirit of a nun who died in the convent. It's haunting my room! I know because I used a ouija board." I stood up. "Father, did any nuns ever die in the chapel?"

He stood abruptly, towering over me and shouted, "You're playing with the devil. Get out of this house!" He pointed to the double doors of the study. "Don't you know suicide is a mortal sin?"

Before I could respond, the housekeeper rushed into the room.

"Is anything wrong, Father?" The woman cowered before the priest.

"Nothing!" He grinned with self-righteousness, sat down, and pointed to the door. "Please show this woman out!"

The housekeeper bowed her head, all but genuflecting to the priest, and held the door open.

As I walked out I heard the priest say one last thing, "You must repent for the redemption of your soul."

I went out the front door and pulled my collar up over my ears to protect them from the wind howling around the corner of the Church. I realized I didn't need a priest that night, I needed a psychic.

Back in Room 7 I got into bed and stared at the ceiling. The continual trauma of the past two years caught up with me.

My mother's illness. Rape. Guilt from the Church. Going for help and being labeled, drugged, and locked up. Michael being drafted. Coming back from the dead. Robert. Pregnancy. Rejection. Miscarriage. The murder on the playground. Being fired. The haunted room and the angry priest.

I was hanging from the edge of a cliff by my fingertips. When I screamed for help, the priest pried my fingers from the ledge and watched, emotionless—as I dropped to my death.

Then shadows and lights in my room moved over me. I lost it that night. In this fit of rage I began to destroy everything in my room. I ran out of the building and headed for the Robert Street Bridge that spanned the Mississippi River. The bridge where Shelly and I had once sat on the top of the arches.

I threw my purse into the gutter and ran as fast as I could to the bridge. I had run out of places to go for help. The psychiatrists would drug me, the Church and my mother would condemn me.

I climbed up on the railing and peered into the murky, churning water of the Mississippi. It beckoned to me, "Jump, Jump, Jump!"

I was about to go off the railing when I felt hands pulling me backwards. A policeman had me by the shoulders. While I fought with him, his partner got out of the police car and came to his aid.

They wrestled me to the ground, handcuffed me, and threw me into the police car. I was taken to the hospital for observation. The handcuffs were removed and I was placed in a padded cell.

When the police were gone a nurse came toward me with a syringe filled with orange liquid. It was Thorazine, the drug I had nearly overdosed on.

"No, No.....I can't take that. I'm allergic to Thorazine. Please, please check my chart. I'm not crazy! I'm not crazy!"

The nurse pressed a buzzer on the wall and two order-lies appeared from nowhere. They twisted my arms back and held me until the shot started working.

I was nineteen years old. Legally they could not keep me locked up for more than seventy-two hours. I planned to leave as soon as I could.

The next morning John, the man from Mickey's Diner, came to visit me. He'd gone to Central Manor to find me. Ellen had told him where I was.

This time I had been assigned a beautiful psychiatrist. When I went into her office I gave her a picture I had painted that morning in art therapy. It was a grassy landscape filled with trees laden with plump, red roses.

The doctor's mouth dropped open when she saw the rose trees.

"If you promise not to hurt yourself I will take you out of the isolation cell."

The psychiatrist spoke in a foreign accent. She had a sweet, feminine voice.

"What do you care?" I said, tugging at the belt on my disposable paper robe.

"You are young. You have your whole life ahead of you."

She reached over and touched my hand and tears gushed over my face. "They....they gave me that drug. Please, don't make me take it again. It scares me!"

"I have read your chart and I don't think you should ever have been on that drug. We have many other kinds we can try!"

"I suppose you think I'm crazy, too. No one believes me about the murder or the haunted room...but it all happened. I'm not hearing voices, either!"

"I didn't say that you were."

The doctor came closer to me and placed her hand gently on my shoulder. "I believe you! And I have something to share with you. It will be our secret."

She had an incredulous look on her face as she spoke.

"Diana, the reason I talk differently than you do is because I'm from Latvia. When I was reading your chart before you came in to see me I was thinking of telling you an old Latvian proverb: 'Life cannot be violins and rose trees.'"

The doctor sat down on a chair next to me and patted my hand.

"And then you gave me this picture that you painted this morning. This picture of rose trees." She smiled at me.

"I don't know what it means. But I don't think you are crazy. We legally have to release you tomorrow, but you can come and see me anytime. Will you?"

I shuffled my feet. "Maybe," I said. But I knew I would never come back to this awful place once I was released, even though that doctor was really nice to me. Maybe all psychiatrists weren't as bad as my first one. But, I was never going near a Catholic Church or psychiatrist again!

CHAPTER 15

"Chapel of Love"

The day I left the hospital John came to get me. Not
feeling welcome at home, I went to John's place. He lived in
two drafty rooms in an old house on Nina Street near St. Paul's
Cathedral.

John did not have a job. He'd only been out of prison
for six months. A few weeks after living together, John and I
had our first fight. I had taken two dollars while he was nap-
ping and gone to the store to buy eggs and pancake mix. I was
going to surprise him and make breakfast.

I set the table and lit a candle, anxious to serve my man.
When he woke up and realized I'd spent two dollars of his
money he was furious with me. I cried, left the house, and took
a bus back to my dad's.

John called me. He said he'd commit suicide if I didn't
come back. I bought the bait. This was the answer to why God
had saved me from suicide. It was my to turn to save someone
else!

April 27, 1969 was a cold, overcast day with snow
lightly falling. John and I took a cab to the Justice of the Peace.

I wore a white miniskirt and John wore a brown west-
ern-cut leisure suit. He called his sister and brother and asked
them to meet us at an office on University Avenue, above
Sorini's Pizza.

Still numb, I followed John's orders like a convert to a
new religion. I told no one that this was my wedding day.

The four of us stood in front of the old Justice of the Peace with the smell of pepperoni wafting up from the pizza place below—(Do you take this sausage to be your lawful wedded husband?) John tape-recorded the service.

When I said "I do," the word *divorce* floated through my head. I dismissed it and followed through with the marriage. I was going to live for my man. Afterwards we went to John's sister's for a dish of vanilla ice cream.

Fourteenth
March
1 9 6 9

Dear Diana:

It was interesting to hear from you again and read of your progress after so long a time. While you apparently tend to concentrate largely on your imperfections, it seems apparent -- just from your letter -- that you are in a far better frame of mind than when I last heard from you.

I notice that the last paragraph of your letter mentions the possibility of marrying the young man you describe as your "only suitor." I strongly advise against this course of action. Marriage, even under the best of circumstances, while it brings great rewards, is also a partly difficult situation, and when one party or the other -- or both -- brings to a marriage serious emotional handicaps, their condition is much more likely to worsen than it is to improve.

To say more here would be presumptuous of me, but I do hope that you find these few ideas of some value.

All good wishes to you.

Cordially,

Steve Allen

My dad helped us out financially the first few months until my generous Uncle Lorin and Aunt Cele hired John to work in their distributing business.

Within a month I was pregnant. The pregnancy had

occurred so close to the miscarriage that I denied I would carry it full term. I wouldn't allow myself to hope for a living baby.

If I miscarried, how could I grieve? I hadn't finished grieving the loss of my innocence, my first baby, the end of my relationship with Michael, Robert, Dad, and my mother.

John did not get involved with my pregnancy and had no desire to be present in the delivery room at the birth of our baby.

On January 13, 1970, I gave birth to Kenneth Dean—a beautiful, perfect son. The responsibilities of motherhood and marriage filled my time. I loved my baby. Kenny had beautiful, curly angel hair and green eyes with long eyelashes.

John and I accepted caretaking duties in a new apartment to get a break in the rent. By the second year John was able to get a job at a canning factory as a maintenance mechanic.

I slowly learned to cook for John. He liked American food: goulash, chili, spaghetti, pot roast. He worked nights and got home at 11:30 P.M. I had a hot meal on the table ready for him, even though Kenny was in bed and I had already eaten. After dinner John laid down in front of the television and I went to bed.

When he thought I was asleep he got up and went out. He'd come back at 3:00 and 4:00 in the morning, go to sleep on the sofa, get up in time for lunch, and then leave for work.

I often would put on lacy negligees and wait for him to come in, hoping to win his attention.

"Where do you go at night?" I begged him to talk to me.

"I just drive around." John threw his coat over the rocking chair. "Look, I was in prison long enough. You ain't gonna lock me up!"

"I don't want to lock you up. Why be married if we never share anything? You don't ever want to make love. You never talk to me. What am I here for? To cook and clean? The only thing we have in common is Kenny."

John picked his coat back up and walked to the door.

"This is worse than prison, and you're nothing but a fucking whore!"

I stepped back and yelled across the living room. "I can't go on like this. It's like living alone. I may as well talk to the wall!"

"You're crazy," John shouted. "You ain't leavin—you could never make it on your own. You're nuts!" He walked out the door and didn't come back until lunch time the next day.

I was the one imprisoned. John didn't want me to learn to drive or to work. He was jealous if I visited with my sister or my old friends. He was even envious of my friendship with his sister and his retarded brother.

In the marriage, John was not physically abusive. He didn't drink, except for an occasional beer. I didn't believe he was seeing another woman because he was so uncomfortable with any kind of touching or intimacy. I didn't think he was with another man, despite his prison time, because he was homophobic. He had no insight into his own nature and no desire to learn to communicate.

Like most women in a bad marriage I blamed myself. I was sure I was doing something wrong. I tried to be the perfect wife, cleaning, cooking, and being sexually alluring. John always insisted I be the initiator of sex. Then he accused me of being oversexed and not being loyal, even though I believed in monogamy in my marriage.

I got tired of begging for love. I needed to love myself so I was not so needy of a man's attention. If John didn't love me, what was the purpose of staying married? He was good to Kenny, but the fighting and the seething anger were not what I wanted my son to grow up with. To stay for my child was to tell him that I didn't matter. After the silence and depression of my childhood, I did not want my son to grow up with the burden of having a martyr for a mother.

If I left, I had no intention of stopping John from seeing his son.

I was imprisoned by John. He became paranoid and accused me of cheating when he was at work. But I had no close friends. I never left the house without him. We never went anywhere but the grocery store or to visit my parents.

Motherhood was my greatest pleasure. Kenny was a bright, happy child who walked at nine months and kept me busy with his constant curiosity. He was intelligent and affectionate. The sad child inside of me learned to have fun with Kenny. When he was a toddler we spent hours together playing and singing, taking walks, drawing, and painting. We were as close as a mother and child can be. That time we shared would hold us together in the darker hours to come.

My mother had become increasingly more lethargic. I was glad she was able to know Kenny. Mom and Dad both loved him. He was a happy baby who loved to be held.

John's ridicule and my isolation led me into a depression. I sometimes called Y.E.S. (Youth Emergency Service) to talk. I wasn't able to trust another therapist, but I wanted to grow again, to be a whole person, and a healthy example for my child.

I continued to correspond with Steve Allen.

Nineteenth
August
1 9 7 0

Dear Diana:

I hope you will forgive me for what must seem an unpardonable delay in responding to your most interesting letter of June 17th. By way of explanation, Jayne and I have been away from the city for quite a few weeks, working in Vancouver, Las Vegas, Michigan, Chicago and New York. Now that we're back, we're faced with a tremendously tall stack of backlogged correspondence, but I think one of these days I may finally catch up with the mail.

I am very pleased indeed that you have succeeded in restoring order to your life after all the tragic difficulties that you have suffered in recent years. There is a degree of tragedy in everyone's life, of course, but you do seem to have had more than your share.

Congratulations on the birth of your beautiful son, Kenneth. Because of your earlier experiences I am sure you will have a greater understanding than do many young mothers today of the vital importance to your own child of daily care and warm physical affection.

I was first married when I was a very wet-behind-the-ears young man, and although I deeply loved my first three sons, I somehow assumed, I suppose, that if their physical needs were provided for, and if they knew their father and mother loved them, growing up would not be especially difficult. How naive I was. Growing to maturity is an enormously difficult process, and perhaps none of us ever totally achieve the ideal of sanity and love to which we all aspire.

All good wishes to the three of you. I am enclosing herewith a couple more items for your personal library.

Keep up the good work.

Cordially,

Steve Allen

I told Kenny often that I loved him. I tried to teach him what I knew about God and what I believed about Christ. I was not able to trust established religions enough to allow them to teach my son, although we sometimes attended Sunday services at the Spiritualist Christian Church.

Kenny was taught that our souls have divine origin, we are part of God. We cannot earn heaven, we can only realize divine love, which is what our highest self is. Then we choose to act for the highest good of all, not because we are afraid of hell as I had been taught, but because we know God.

Kenny and I prayed together before he went to sleep. We prayed for guidance, not for our souls to be taken in our sleep. We prayed for protection in life from sorrow and fear. We asked for answers, guidance, miracles, and healing. I no longer believed that God spoke to a few special clergy or saints. I began to know God spoke to everyone, every day, through people, intuition, and healing love.

Kenny learned how the powerful had murdered Jesus

and how Jesus allowed the crucifixion so that he could return in Spirit and prove there is no death. I taught Kenny from my new beliefs about celebrating the transition of the soul back to God, rather than the celebration of the crucifixion and death of Christ's body. The Church glorified suffering and pain. Christ desired to heal the world, not to bring more pain upon it. His example was of love, equality, non-conformity, and freedom of Spirit, which is always safe, even in "death," in the hand of God. All the patriarchal rules and fables built around Christ's life have been distorted and abused to control people with fear and guilt.

I never told my child that people who did not believe in Jesus would go to hell. The Church has created God in man's egotistical image with that lie. God is not some vain dictator requiring our worship. In the same way I love my child when he says, "I hate you," God must love us no less.

It was much easier to love people when I gave the judgement back to God. It was good to stop measuring everyone by their sins.

I began to realize that everyone on earth is on a spiritual journey, whether they know it or not. Some choose to walk with their eyes open and others with their eyes shut. There are advantages to both ways of walking.

When the denial of my mismatched marriage ended, I cried a lot and started to plan a future without John. But how? I had no skills and only a high school education. The only success experience I had in my life was motherhood. The thought of leaving Kenny while I went to some menial job was not easy to consider. John was a good provider, but I had to beg for necessities like underwear and feminine products.

I had only wanted two things from a husband back then. I wanted him to talk to me and to take a bath. It was in John's favor that I had hardly any sense of smell. John did not like to take baths. I eventually discovered that he was not taking showers at work as he said he did after his shift. It got so bad that I counted a three-week period he went without bathing. I felt like I was raising another child. I started to push the grocery cart ahead of me in the supermarket, afraid people would think he was my husband. He was a chain smoker and looked much older than thirty-six. People said they thought he was my father.

I was twenty-three years old and Kenny two-and-a-half, when I found lice eggs on his beautiful eyelashes and in his blonde curly hair. It made me repulsed and furious at John. Even after the doctor assured me it was gone, I had nightmares about it and thought I saw lice everywhere! Every speck of dust and dirt seemed to crawl. I took enough baths to make up for the ones John never took. I knew that lice was easily trans-ferred, but this was no accident, this was John's fault and he knew it. He still went out nights and I had no idea where he was going. I did not want to sleep with him towards the end because I worried he might give me a sexually transmitted disease. John continually told me I was crazy and that I would never leave him because I was mentally ill.

I cherished the letters from Steve Allen, my mentor. He continued to write me letters throughout the 1970's and sent me more of his books. I read all his children's books to Kenny who begged me to read *Princess Snip Snip and the Puppykittens* over and over and over.

Twenty-Seventh
March
1 9 7 4

Dear Diana:

How nice to hear from you again.

I enjoyed seeing the beautiful snapshot of you and your family. Thanks, too, for letting me see the copy of the fine sketch you did, and particularly for letting me read your poems, which I think are fine and sensitive.

Keep up the good work.

Forgive me for not being absolutely certain whether I've earlier sent you a copy of my latest book, "Princess Snip Snip and the Puppykittens."

If I have, well, now you have two autographed copies.

All good wishes to you and your fine family.

Cordially,

Steve Allen

I watched television to escape from my marital problems. At that time, *The Phil Donahue Show* was the only talk show on television. Phil had authors and psychologists on his television show talking about women's lives. The more I watched his program, the more I saw courageous women who were not afraid to get divorced and start a new life on their own. As isolated as I was, there was no other place for me to see women role models. I cannot be sure if I would ever have left John had I not watched Phil Donahue. To this day, when others ridicule talk shows for sensationalism, I remember the empowering messages I learned while imprisoned in my home. Phil Donahue, like Steve Allen, had a great respect for women as whole beings, with intelligence and value. Phil Donahue was not afraid to let people know that Catholicism had its flaws. He was the first person on television to expose America's social, political, and moral hypocrisy. Women of the baby boom generation know the positive influence he had in changing our lives for the better.

About the time I was ready to give up on my marriage, my brothers Peter and Terry were giving instructions in Transcendental Meditation, the relaxation technique they had learned in India from Maharishi Mahesh. TM was just becoming popular in the United States and my brothers were the first teachers in Minnesota.

When the Beatles and Mia Farrow were studying in India with Maharishi, the movement became very popular. I remember seeing Maharishi on television. He never became defensive or angry with people who mocked him. His humility and joy were apparent. Many other celebrities also began to practice TM in those years like Joe Namath, Clint Eastwood, and Merv Griffin. I believe that many of the Beatles songs were influenced by their spiritual seeking in those years.

Many other gurus would ride to fame in the trail of TM's success. I do not know what the others were teaching, but I can testify that my practice of TM affected my mental outlook quicker than any therapy could have, or did. I began to practice for twenty minutes twice a day.

Within a month of starting TM, I had stopped crying. I was more confident and less dependent on John's opinion for my self-esteem. TM worked, but not simply because I believed in it. I had no understanding of it and no belief about it. I tried it out of respect for my brothers and with the hope that I might be less depressed.

I did not join the meditation community that grew up around TM. After being Catholic, I had an aversion to group conformity. What I loved about meditation was that I could take it with me and never had to join the organization or even associate with other meditators, as some preferred.

Once I learned to meditate I never had to talk about it again if I chose not to. I could just use it to enhance my self-knowledge and my spiritual growth. I did not have to espouse any dogma or become vegetarian or join a religion. TM was a relaxation practice, like any meditation, that allowed me to find the source of strength and support within. This was not contradictory with the words of Christ. In fact, it was a way of finding "the Kingdom of God within" that Christ had promised us if we would seek it. The Church had never given us enough empowerment to say we could find this in ourselves. The Church always emphasized the clergy and pope, who knew God in a way the sinner could not.

At first meditation was unnerving. When I sat down to relax, I was restless and my mind wandered on everyday things—what to fix for supper, whether I needed a hair cut, if I should learn to drive.

As I became more still and accustomed to twenty-minute meditations, I learned to quiet my thoughts and then I began to experience exactly what Christ had told us of the place in all of us where divinity resides. I knew then that our soul is not a separate part of God, but one with it, and we cannot feel it when we are out in the dense energy of the world.

Many feelings of anger and thoughts of betrayal surfaced. I tried to release them, not to hang on to them. I realized that God is here now to know, not in some distant heaven that we have to suffer to get to, nor some unachievable height destined only for the chosen few.

The more frequently I meditated, the more often I could silence my mind enough to sink to the depth of my being and experience peace and the Light of God that filled the silence. It gave me a sense of security. No matter what happened in life, nothing, not even a communist invasion, could take this from me. It was a gift, a tool that would help me survive. I had no idea of the horrific events that were to follow and how much more I would need meditation than I did when I started it.

CHAPTER 16

"The Sounds of Silence"

By early 1972 my mother's health had deteriorated. The effect of liberally prescribed narcotics and radiation damage had taken their toll. Mom told the family over the years to be sure and "pull the plug" if she ever "blew a fuse."

Her muscles had atrophied from lack of use, after spending years in bed. Her body, normally small, was bloated, her face pale and swollen. She was often incoherent. Sometimes she could not keep her tongue in her mouth. It appeared that something had finally snapped.

Mom had once had beautiful, perfect white teeth. She used to tell us they were "at the top of the dentist's whiteness scale." One week, my mother had complained that her teeth hurt her. Mysteriously, she went into the hospital and a few days later came home with no teeth. She tried to wear dentures, but they did not fit correctly. She wandered around the house in her jelly-stained robe, toothless—this woman who had once been so beautiful.

When her teeth were removed she seemed to lose all hope of recovering her beauty. Taking away her perfect smile had removed the final hope that she would ever leave the house. Medically, her teeth did not need to be removed. The dentist had taken them out following her orders, in much the same way the doctor had indiscriminately prescribed her drugs.

The more incoherent Mom became, the more often she

said she had cancer and other catastrophic illnesses she had read about. Because of her history of medical abuse, I understood why she refused to see a physician, although I never knew what was really wrong with my mother. I have no doubt she suffered physically and mentally. But it was before chemical dependency from prescription drugs was understood and long before people began questioning doctors.

Through the years Mom talked about working as a registered nurse, about the blundering of surgeons she'd seen when she was a surgical nurse. She had seen more than her share of fatal mistakes. Her past was continually eating away at her. If she had gone to work outside the home and not sacrificed herself for her children, she might have seen how the world had changed in the thirty years since she had left nursing, but she was still in the old world where women were not allowed to have a career and children. She still believed that "silence is golden." But I could feel something else—something that permeated her being. It was a sadness I could feel, a sadness that contradicted her words, her constant talk of God and cheerfulness. It was a demon that locked her lips.

By the time I was twenty-three I had spent most of my life expecting my mother to die, because she always said she was dying. I was numb to the fact she would ever die.

At my parents' house one quiet summer afternoon my mom and I sat in the living room, while Kenny napped on the sofa. Mom seemed extremely lethargic. Her lips were parched and her speech was slow and labored. It reminded me of the limbo I had been in while on Thorazine, when I could not communicate what I was thinking or feeling.

I was at my father's desk in the living room looking at the mail and paging through his *National Geographic Magazine* when my eyes wandered over the framed photos on his desk. I picked up one taken several years before at our house. In the photo Mother was sitting on the sofa with four nuns, all dressed in black habits. I remembered this day. I was in high school and she told me they had worked with her when she was a nurse in Ladysmith, Wisconsin.

I remembered seeing the name of Sister Mary Lucy written in several of Mom's old prayer books and hymnals, even the words S.M. Lucy were carved in the wooden darning egg she used when she mended our socks.

I went over to where Mom was resting on a recliner with her eyes half-shut and placed my hand on her arm, "Mom? Mom?" I said quietly.

She opened her eyes and replied, "Yes, Dear?" I put the photo in front of her. "Which one of the nuns in this photo is your friend, Sister Lucy?"

She smiled a half-smile and answered with one word, "Me."

"Right," I said sarcastically. "Now really, Mom, tell me which nun was sister Lucy. You have all her books, she must have been your best friend...." She looked at me and smiled again. Before she had "Me" out of her mouth for the second time, I finally understood. The clues had been around me all my life, but I had never picked up on them. *My mother had been a nun.*

"NO. . . you're kidding, right?" I asked, astonished. But she didn't answer. Mother's eyes had closed shut and she was snoring loudly. She was in one of those deep, drug-induced stupors that no one could wake her from. Sometimes she slept for sixteen hours at a time. We had gotten used to this at the house.

I stood in the living room staring at my mother. Tears filled my eyes. "God, why? Why would you keep this from me? I'm your daughter!" Memories of childhood rushed to the front of my mind, fighting each other to reach my consciousness. No wonder. No wonder she had reacted so hysterically when she found out I was pregnant.

No wonder she told me it was better to be killed than raped. The tears felt warm on my face as they fell over my chin onto my T-shirt. There was an aching in my heart as I tried to examine each memory crowding in on me.

I recalled a day when Donna and I were young. Mom had taken us downtown on the bus in late afternoon to see a

matinee show at the Orpheum Theatre, starring Audrey
Hepburn, called *The Nun's Story*.

I remembered the end of the movie so well. The mis-
sionary nun took off her nun's habit and left the convent. My
sister and I were very happy because the beautiful nun was
going to marry a handsome man. I became aware suddenly that
my mother had taken a flowered handkerchief out of her purse
and dabbed her eyes with it. She was crying. No matter how
fast she wiped away the tears, they kept coming.

"What's the matter, Mommy, are you sick?"

"No, Dear, I just have a cold. Why don't you girls go
wait in the lobby for your father to come and pick us up. I have
to go to the ladies room."

While Mother was in the bathroom, we sat on the tufted
velvet bench to wait for Daddy to pick us up from the theatre. I
knew my mother was lying. She stayed in the bathroom for a
very long time, hiding her tears from her daughters. I had
received the worst message of silence. I could not be trusted
with the truth.

If only I had known! My entire life would have been
different.

I was so angry that my father and my mother had kept
their vow of silence not to tell their children the truth. We had
it drilled into us from our birth never to tell a lie, but this
deception was worse than a lie. I had felt my mother's pain so
often and believed that she suffered because I was a bad little
girl who had caused her pain. She was my role model, the
woman who taught me who God was. She was so much a part
of me that I did not know where my mother ended and I began.

Had I known that she had been a nun, I might never
have taken her indifference so personally after I became pregnant.

Had I known she had been a nun, I might have realized
why she believed virginity mattered so much. Of course, she
had been a "Bride of Christ!"

I had taken my own vows of silence to tell no one I was
raped. I blamed myself for not letting myself be killed rather
than giving in to Steve's demands.

Had I known my mother had been a nun, I might never have taken an overdose. I still did not understand why God had saved me.

Mother had become a recluse. She may as well have been locked in a convent. She was obsessed with religion. She had no close women friends, no life outside of her own lost world of guilt, her own perpetual suffering which she offered up to God as penance.

I, too, had taken the role of martyr. My parents' secret about my mother's seven years in the convent had altered my life, the way the secret of alcoholism alters children of alcoholics. We lived in crisis with her prescription drug addiction and her religious fervor. I did not know what life without fear was. I was burdened with the fear of losing my soul to the devil, burdened with the fear of losing my mother to death because of an illness I believed my birth had caused.

Fear and Guilt. The cornerstones of the Church. I promised my child at that moment that I would never lie to him. I would never deceive him with silence. When I was angry at John or someone else I always explained to Kenny that it was not him I was angry with. I had received the message as a child that the world was a terrible place and we were powerless in it. All we could do was suffer until we died and hope that heaven was better, if we had few enough sins to win it.

I would give him the truth and teach him that he was strong enough and protected enough to handle whatever life offered him on his path.

He would not feel weak and powerless in a world of evil and suffering.

The endless memories kept circling through my brain.

It explained why my mother did not sleep with my father. It was the reason she only believed in sex for procreation. The reason she believed suffering was admirable. It was the reason she did not seem to appreciate my father's loyalty and affection towards her. How could he compete with Jesus? It was the reason she had done "civil baptism" on fetuses.

Her words haunted me, "Better to kill you than rape you." . . . "Better to kill you than rape you."

Along with this revelation, this constant remembering of events that suddenly made sense, was the total indifference of my family. None of them thought it was important to know that my mother had been a nun. It took me many years to understand why. Of course my brothers could not have been affected by my mother in the same way. They were all older and were out of the house for a large part of her worst years of suffering and delusion. They were not taught what girls had been taught.

Woman saints who martyred themselves for their virginity were praised in school, but there were no men saints revered for virginity. Mother was my role model, not theirs. I had always thought I would go to bed one day, turn to the wall, and give up on life as she had.

I took my mother's feelings as my own. I felt everything she felt. Eventually my search for myself through my mother brought me greater understanding.

I learned that my mother had given me the middle name Louise because it had been her best friend's name in the convent. She had also coerced me into taking the name of Lucy for my confirmation name. I wanted the name Rose. Lucy was her name as a nun. From the beginning there was a strong bond between us. I believe that we were closer for a reason.

Saint Lucy was the saint who discovered she had a suitor who loved her beautiful eyes, so she plucked her eyes out to ensure her virginity.

Thirty years later, of course, I believe my mother's choice was part of my life plan, the script we had agreed upon with God to fulfill. I had to live through the experiences in order to understand my mother's pain and be able to write this book. This was the script my mother and I had been given and we both played our lines to the end.

This was the true beginning of my spiritual search. Not

to find a religion, but to find God. I knew after meditating that God was not in some stale church. I knew that God had not abandoned me through all my mistakes. In fact, God was not letting me out of this world until I had done whatever it was God had saved me for.

Even though I had tried to take my own life. I had never stopped believing in God. I just wanted unity on the other side, where I knew it would be better than in this violent world.

I had been angry with God for not making my mother well, for not answering my prayers as a child.

As I came to believe in the importance of free will in my life, I started to understand that God had not healed my mother because my mother did not want to be healed. She believed as she had been taught, that suffering was the path to heaven. God could not take away her pain as long as she believed that pain was her ticket to heaven. It was a terrible dichotomy that she never recovered from.

I began to understand how that belief had also sabotaged my own happiness. I had so much guilt that whenever I had hope or joy or love I stopped it. How could I be happy when suffering was Godly and the way to heaven?

Knowing my mother had been a nun was a revelation that turned my life around. I had never gotten over the guilt of the rape and the guilt of the suicide attempt and the guilt of Susan Merek's death. I believed because I was the one who wanted to die, I was the one God should have taken. It would have been a perfect ending. My mother would have been happy if I went to heaven as a martyr and Susan Merek would have been alive.

But now I could see that my mother, who had prayed to die all my life, who had begged for God to take her, had been suffering from the same deadly guilt that I had. She never had resolved leaving the convent. I had to find out more, even though my father refused to talk about it saying, "It's in the past. What does it have to do with you?"

He could not see its effect on me. Not only could I now understand my mother, I could forgive her. She had been the victim of religion. And I had been the victim of religion. We had suffered the same fate. I could love my mother and maybe someday when I finished grieving my childhood, I would be able to love myself.

CHAPTER 17

"Don't Make Me Over"

Fourteenth
December
1 9 7 3

Dear Diana:

I hope the present Christmas season is a happy
one for you and your fine family.

All good wishes to you.

Cordially,

Steve Allen

     Like many couples starting a divorce, John and I tried
to reconcile our differences amicably. Not knowing how I
could support Kenny alone, I went back and forth in my mind
whether to leave John or try again.

     I accepted a job as a kitchen aide in a nursing home
where I washed dishes and helped prepare and serve breakfast.
When I started working my self-esteem was nonexistent. I
wore a uniform stained with strained food fed to the toothless
patients and a hairnet to keep my hair from getting into the
food. I continued to practice Transcendental Meditation, a
constant renewal, and began writing poetry, and sketching.

Mom's health was deteriorating. Sometimes she could not control her tongue and it hung outside her mouth. She slept most of the time. The drugs had finally blown a fuse. But we pretended everything was okay, as usual.

The last large meal I prepared for John and my relatives together was Thanksgiving, 1972. Dad got Mom out of bed, put a coat on her and took her to our duplex for the day. She said she had a cold and coughed throughout the meal.

While I was cleaning up the dishes after dinner, Mom shuffled into the kitchen. I remember her saying, "You kids don't need me anymore." I just smiled and led Mom back to the sofa in the living room. I could not imagine what prompted her to say that. We had not needed her since we were children.

She still refused to talk about having been a nun.

Monday morning my brother Peter called to tell me the news. Mother had died in her sleep. Dad found her in the morning.

An autopsy was performed. Mom had pneumonia. It was odd because she had often said she had cancer or some other catastrophic illness which never materialized. Then to have her die of pneumonia, just seemed unreal.

Expecting my mother to die throughout most of my life, it was harder to believe now that she was really gone. It was a long winter, but I took comfort in the belief that now, finally, Mom had some peace.

Finally Spring arrived. At the nursing home, employees began to meet outside on the patio during coffee break. David, a handsome male nurse, sometimes sat next to me and talked. He was clean and smelled wonderful. He had thoughts, ideas, and feelings! And he listened! He validated me. He didn't treat me as though I were crazy or sinful.

During that time I began to feel that I was a writer. One of the editors for the local *Sun* newspapers, had started a poetry column and asked for submissions. She published several of my poems. The *St. Paul Pioneer Press* published an essay I'd written on world peace. They even sent a reporter to my house to take my picture. I received wonderful letters from readers who liked my story. I proudly shared these writings with David.

I had been lonely and empty for so long. With David listening, love poured into my heart like water into a dry fountain. He was the first man I had ever had for a friend. Roberta Flack's song, "The First Time Ever I Saw Your Face" was popular. I bought the record and played it over and over. David could not have known how much those ten-minute breaks meant to me. My heart was opening again and he was the catalyst. I loved David. I loved just seeing his face.

I was only twenty-fours years old. David's presence stirred a physical desire in me that had been dormant since I married John. I fantasized trapping him alone in the elevator and embracing him. I knew it was only my fantasy. David was happily married. But once I felt that love again, I could no longer deny the truth. I did not love John. It was a risk to leave John in the hope that someone might give me the kind of love I felt for David. I knew, after five years, I had to take that risk.

I had changed since I'd left home and married John. But John had not changed at all.

It was not so much John's inability to give love as it was his inability to receive the love I had to give that made my love impotent and my heart ache.

In an effort to keep me, John bought me a new diamond wedding ring and a wonderful house. But it wasn't enough. Material things could not hold me. I wanted my integrity back. He finally agreed to give me a divorce.

At first, John had agreed to everything. We even went to the Divorce Education Association to learn how to file our own papers so we could save money. John paid the down payment on a one-bedroom apartment I moved into with Kenny in the Midway area of St. Paul.

I had been hired as a clerk-typist in a building just

across the parking lot, earning minimum wage. There was an in-house daycare in my apartment building.

John had spent five years telling me I was crazy and weak. He was sure I'd be begging him to take me back before the first week was over—but I wanted my independence. I had asked for minimal child support and offered liberal visitation. I didn't even try to get the house because I had no way of affording a mortgage payment.

I never looked back. I loved my freedom. I could talk to people again and be myself without being ridiculed.

The most painful part was leaving Kenny at the daycare. The first day I had to leave him, he hung onto my arm pleading with me, "Don't go, Mommy! Mommy, don't leave me!"

The teacher pulled him away from me and I said, "Mommy has to go to work. I love you, Kenny." As I walked away from the door I saw his little four-year-old face turning red. Kenny screamed as loud as he could. The daycare teacher held him back, restraining his flailing arms.

I choked back the tears. As I walked out the revolving door onto the sidewalk I cried, "My baby, my baby..."

I worked in the Central Medical Office Building across the parking lot from our apartment high-rise as a clerk-typist for the board of nursing. They paid me $3.20 an hour.

When I got home from the first day on the job, Kenny was sitting in a little wicker chair by the door watching for me. His eyes were red and puffy from crying. He grabbed onto me so tightly, I wanted to quit my job that minute. "Mommy, don't ever leave me again."

"I love you, Tiger. Mommy didn't leave you." There was no way I could make him understand why I couldn't just be his mommy for every minute, like before. I lifted him up in my arms. He sobbed all the way back to the apartment. We made chocolate chip cookies to cheer ourselves up.

After three weeks I received my first check. John finally realized that I had no intention of returning to him. He called and threatened suicide, the way he had before we were married. But I could no longer take responsibility for his life.

When that didn't work, John started on a campaign of death threats against me, my family, and even Kenny, calling throughout the night.

"I dug a hole big enough for the three of us. Stop the divorce or I'll kill us all. You're not getting Kenny. You're not going to ever have anything as long as I'm alive!"

I called the police.

"Did anyone else hear the threat, Ma'am?"

"No, but I'm afraid. He's angry. He means it! He has a criminal record!"

"Sorry, Ma'am, but it's what we call a domestic. I'll make out a report, but we can't do anything until he acts on the threat."

"Even though he has a prison record?"

"No, we can't use anything he's done in the past."

I had learned the first rule in a long, hard lesson. Justice had nothing to do with the law. If the police had a body or a witness I might get a response. I had no protection. The average person obeyed the law because he or she feared getting caught. But John had been in prison long enough to know that getting punished for anything you did to your "property—your wife or child" was not likely.

Then John refused to sign the divorce papers. I had to get my own attorney. I had no money.

CHAPTER 18

"Hit The Road, Jack"

I contacted the Legal Aid Society and they assigned me an attorney named Mr. Benson. I explained to him that I had no money and warned him of John's incarceration and recent death threats. The attorney informed us that he took an occasional legal aid case and I would be charged only for the filing fees. He was friendly and talkative, much like a skilled salesman.

My attorney thought I should get the house. Since we had had it for only six months and I couldn't afford the payments, I preferred to forfeit the house to John. I only wanted minimal child support. I didn't want to anger John further.

"Most men threaten when their wife leaves. Your husband will get over it." Mr. Benson wouldn't acknowledge my fear and I was getting used to the indifference of authority. I had no other choice.

I explained to Mr. Benson that our safety was more important than any monetary settlement. John had nothing of value. All I wanted was my independence.

"I just want a divorce as soon as I can get one so I can go on with my life."

Assuring me he would begin the paperwork, Mr. Benson finished the interview and advised me to keep detailed notes of any harassment that occurred.

Several times, day and night, the phone rang. When I picked it up the caller said nothing. I hung up.

When I tried to call out ten minutes later, the phone was

dead. Whoever had made the call, kept the receiver off the hook, making it impossible for me to call out or to receive a call from anyone else.

I recorded the incessant phone calls and hangups and finally took the phone off the hook to get some sleep. I needed an unlisted phone number, regardless of what it cost. The little money I had left wouldn't last long. I felt trapped.

Even though I lived in a security building I knew John could easily walk in behind someone who had used their ID card to open the door. There was no way I could call the police, my attorney, or family when he'd left the phone off the hook. Of course, I couldn't prove John made the calls when he didn't talk.

Sometimes when I answered, John did talk. He would say, "I'm going to kill your whole fucking family!" and then he'd hang up.

John had not acted on his threats, but the harassment began to wear on me. Even if his intention was not to kill me, he could trap me in my own apartment. It prevented me from going on with my life. Without any money or a car I was immobilized. Kenny sensed anxiety and became even more fearful of leaving me when I took him to the daycare center before I went to school.

I informed the daycare of the situation and advised them not to allow anyone but me to pick Kenny up, especially not his father. They were sympathetic and supportive.

I tried to concentrate on what I could control and let the rest go. If I hid in my apartment, John would have succeeded in controlling me. I had to let him know that I was not going to be intimidated.

I learned that John was befriending my family in an effort to discredit me. He tried to convince them that I was being revengeful and imagining the harassment, that I'd gone crazy. At first, because of my behavior during my teen years, they were inclined to believe him. It was very painful to have him use this against me. After all, I had changed considerably. I was no longer unstable and I was not overreacting.

If John could convince my own family that I was losing it, how could I convince them that he was lying? It was so obvious to me. He wasn't being harassed. I was.

At the same time he was manipulating my family, he was telling me he planned to kill them. It was enough to make me crazy. But I wanted to live. It didn't matter what anyone thought. In several calls he said he planned to destroy my father's house. He said he was going to set fire to the house we'd owned and say that I did it. I started having dreams that our house was on fire, and I remembered what John had told me shortly after we were married. When he was an adolescent he'd been paid more than once to set fire to warehouses and businesses so the owners could collect the insurance. He had never been caught or convicted for arson. And I could tell he was proud of getting away with it.

I called the police department and had them make a record of every call, as my attorney had advised.

Frequently, I took the phone off the hook, resting the receiver on the table but then I really felt trapped. I worried about something happening to my family and no one being able to reach me.

When I left for work in the morning John was waiting outside in his car for me. He drove beside me and behind me as I walked across the long parking lot. I tried to look straight ahead, ignoring him, refusing to respond to his violent threats. "Hey, whore! Hey, bitch, whore. I'm going to kill you and your whole fuckin' family. Whore! You hear me!"

I prayed silently, the Spiritualist prayer, "Light of God, Surround me. Nothing but good shall come to me...(and the hardest part to say)...Nothing but good shall go from me."

I was already exhausted when I started work from sleepless nights and because my back muscles had tightened up from anticipating a knife or bullet in the back.

John was there when I left the office, but he was less vocal because more witnesses were nearby. It became apparent he had quit his job to dedicate himself full time to harassing me and to avoid paying child support.

Kenny had nightmares, wetting his pants, and crying at night. He was afraid to stay in his bedroom alone and wanted to sleep with me on the sofabed to be sure I didn't leave him.

John had never harmed Kenny when we were married or abused me physically. I was shocked that he didn't see or care how his threats affected Kenny. He was obsessed with revenge, with keeping me from going on with my life.

Sometimes on the phone, I tried to talk with him, to convince him that it was futile to continue harassing me. He only became angrier and I became more frustrated. When he followed me in his car, I forced myself to look away, never to make eye contact. Sometimes Tyrone, a guard at the front desk of the apartment building, walked me to work. He was one of my few friends.

I called to get my phone number changed and asked about getting it tapped so I could record his threats. The phone company informed me the tapping would occur only if the police requested it and it would cost me a new service fee to get an unlisted number. But the police said they wanted no part of a domestic.

That week I received a box of Fanny Farmer chocolates in the mail. The box was wrapped in brown paper. A small card was enclosed signed in crooked print, "From the Girls." The sealed cellophane had been removed from the candy box. In the center of the box several paper cups had been taken out and replaced with a large irregular-shaped piece of homemade fudge filled with tiny white specks, suggesting it had been tampered with—poisoned!

Kenny wanted a chocolate. I had to stop him from eating any. A few days later I received an elaborate sympathy card sentimentally wishing my recovery from the death of a beloved family member and signed by "a friend."

As always when I called to report it to the attorney and police, I was advised that I could not prove the candy or card had been sent by John. Without proof, their hands were tied. I implored the attorney to speed up the restraining order.

John started to drive closer behind me and to rev the

engine as I walked across the parking lot, yelling obscenities and threats, "Whore. Give up. You are fuckin' nuts. Nobody believes you, not even your family!"

John told me that he had checked something on my dad's car for him and tampered with it. "Your old man is never getting to the airport alive." I knew Dad was leaving that week for California on a business trip. Dad had survived heart surgery, but the stress of death threats was interfering with his continued healing.

One Friday after a month of constant stalking, John followed me on foot as I walked through the parking lot to work. He had a handgun. I ran into the building. He chased me. I escaped into the elevator and went down to the floor where I worked. When I got out, John was already in the hall pointing the gun at me. I made it into the office and John didn't follow me because there were witnesses inside.

Frightened and out of breath, I ran into the cubicle of a secretary I worked with and collapsed into a chair next to her desk. "He has a gun," I blurted, trying to catch my breath. I started to choke on the tears as I explained what had happened. After I'd calmed down I went into an empty office and called the police and my attorney. I still had not received a restraining order. The lawyer was out, but I left a message with his secretary, reminding him that I needed the restraining order. She told me he had tried to reach me by phone, that the initial papers had been completed and needed my signature. I explained the phone harassment, that I was unable to call out.

Of course, there were no witnesses. A few people had been in the lobby when I ran into the building, but no one had seen the gun. He'd hidden it under his jacket. I had to calm down. My heart pounded so rapidly it felt like it was going to leap out of my chest. I prayed and went back to my desk to try and type envelopes. I had to keep this job. It was all I had.

My thoughts were spinning. Who would take care of Kenny if he did kill me? Would he murder me and my son? He was an ex-felon. It was illegal for him to own a gun.

That afternoon a well-dressed young man came into the

office and served me legal papers. John was countersuing for divorce. Included in the papers was a request for custody and a court order restraining me from harassing John or making any false statements regarding harassment.

It was a bizarre joke, a Woody Allen movie. This couldn't be happening. I was the victim, not him! By the end of the day everyone in the office knew I was being harassed.

CHAPTER 19

"Smoke Gets In Your Eyes"

That night I asked my brother, who was living at Dad's house, to come and get me and Kenny. I needed to get away. At Dad's I was jumpy. Whenever the phone rang I knew it was John. I kept looking out the window to be sure his car was not cruising by. How could I live a normal life with this constant fear? John did not come around on Saturday.

The next day my sister convinced me to take Kenny and go to the beach. I felt safer in a crowd than when I was alone. Up until now John had avoided taking any action in front of witnesses. We parked the car and started walking toward the beach. All of a sudden I heard John yelling at me from behind us. I turned to look. He was not in his own car, but was driving a brown car I'd never seen before. Kenny held my hand tightly as John shouted to me.

"I'm going to destroy your dad's house. I'll kill your whole fucking family. I mean it this time!"

"Get away from me!" I yelled.

A driver behind John's car tried to get by and blared his horn.

John flipped him the finger and drove off.

I was determined not to let John control me. Still shaken, we walked to the beach and laid out our things. I sat down fighting back the tears and tried to encourage Kenny to play in the water. He didn't want to leave my side. How was it affecting Kenny to hear his father threaten to kill us? I had to consciously fight the despair that descended on me. I felt helpless to protect us. I could only concentrate on what I could control. I had to take each day as it came, not knowing if it would be our last. I had to try and visualize a future, even though the world had turned its back on me.

John's phone calls resumed as soon as I returned to my dad's house. Dad was in California. Feeling responsible for endangering my family, I asked my brother Terry to take Kenny and me back to the apartment. I couldn't get away from John. He was obsessed with following me. At least at the apartment we had a security door and a guard in the lobby.

That night, I lay awake with Kenny sleeping next to me, praying, thinking, crying—but not sleeping. I worried about my brother and my father's house.

At approximately 2:30 A.M. the phone rang. Thinking it might be Terry, I answered it.

"Your dad's house is on fire. Terry is trapped inside the burning house." It was John. He laughed and hung up the phone. I hoped to God he was only bluffing. I had to call my brother before John called back and tied up my phone line. I dialed my father's phone number. A tape-recorded voice came on the line, "I'm sorry. The number you have reached is out of service."

I called my brother Peter and asked him to please go to Dad's house and check on Terry. He lived closer than I did. I told him I'd get a cab and meet him there.

I locked up the apartment and carried Kenny, who was still asleep, into the elevator and down to the lobby. Only five minutes had passed when a yellow cab pulled up in front of the high-rise. I hurried out and opened the back door. As I got into the cab, I froze. John was sitting on the other side of the back seat grinning. I couldn't tell if he had the gun.

Before I could respond, he had given the cabby my father's address and the driver pulled the taxi out into the darkness.

"Look, I heard about the fire on the police radio." John talked fast, trying to get out of it.

I held onto the arm rest with one hand and held Kenny tightly on my lap with the other. The cab made its way though the dark, empty streets. The driver was taking back streets, far out of the way. I thought he must be taking a longer way to increase the cost of the fare.

I stared out into the dark night, caught in limbo and began to wonder if the driver was in on this with John. It was especially eerie when he turned into the parkway and passed Duluth Playground, where Susan Merek had been murdered.

We finally made it to York Avenue. I could see my childhood home smoldering. Three fire trucks lined the drive-way. Smoked drifted out of the broken windows.

As I got out of the cab with Kenny I heard John say in a muffled voice, "You can't prove anything." I ignored him and headed for the driveway. Kenny was awake and struggling to get down.

Where was Terry?

As two of the fire trucks pulled out of the driveway, I saw him by the garage talking to the fire marshall. I set Kenny down, took his hand, and ran to my brother.

As I reached the fire marshall's car I saw Peter drive up to the curb. The cab left, with John in it.

"Terry, are you okay?" I interrupted the fire marshall.

"Yeah, I'm alive. I woke up to the sound of water boiling in the radiator. The phone was dead so I ran next door to call the fire department."

The fire marshall took off his helmet and wiped his brow.

"He was lucky he got out. The fire was damn close to the gas water heater. Another ten minutes and the place would have blown. I'll be back in the daylight to finish the investigation. I'd stay out of the basement until it gets aired out." The fire marshall left the scene.

The acid smell of charred wood filled the air. You could taste it. We went inside the smoky living room.

Terry's voice trembled as he told us what had happened.

After being awakened by the sound of water boiling in the radiator, he smelled smoke. He went downstairs, through the kitchen, and touched the doorknob leading to the basement but it was too hot to hold onto. Black smoke poured out from under the door. He tried the phone, but the line was dead.

"How did you know about the fire?" Terry looked at Pete and then at me.

"John called me and said you were trapped inside. I called Pete and got a cab over here."

"Mommy, I have to go potty."

"Go ahead, honey," Kenny left my side and went into the bathroom.

"John set it." I whispered to keep Kenny from hearing. "I know he did. He threatened to destroy the house when I was at the lake today."

"Oh, God." Terry backed up and sat down on the sofa. "The fire marshall told me there was a box full of flammable materials, paint thinner and old paint cans, in the middle of the basement. Right where John had stored your things when you moved out of your house."

"Yeah, but how did he get in?" Pete asked.

"It's easy enough to climb through the basement window," I answered. "I did it last Spring when I forgot my key. Besides, John's a locksmith, remember? How did he know the house was on fire if he didn't set it?"

We looked at one another.

Kenny came out of the bathroom rubbing his eyes.

"My eyes hurt, Mommy."

"I know, dear, it's the smoke."

I asked Terry to stay at our apartment that night, but he couldn't.

"I can't leave the house open like this. I'll have to board up the broken windows tomorrow. I'll stay in the living room for the night!"

I was afraid for him but I couldn't convince him to leave. Peter gave Kenny and me a ride back home. I had to go to work in a few hours. I was jittery and sick to my stomach.

It was a miracle Terry had survived.

I stayed awake all night. The next morning I forced myself to drop Kenny off at the daycare and go to work. I started across the parking lot expecting to be shot in the back. John drove up behind me, speeding up. I thought he was going to run me over.

He yelled out the window, "Hey, whore, I'm going to kill your father and get away with it, like I got away with setting his house on fire!" As I made it to the sidewalk curb, he turned and drove away.

I ran into work where I called and left messages for the police, my attorney, and the fire marshall to report John's admission of arson.

The police detective called back first, then my attorney, and finally the fire marshall. They all responded with the same clinical objectivity.

"Did anyone else hear him besides you?" As if I didn't count.

"It won't hold up. It's your word against his."

I tried to make them understand, "But it was attempted murder. My brother got out just in time. John told me he did it. He said he was going to murder my family and get away with it. It's my father's house!"

Nothing I said mattered. I began to believe that even if my brother had died, they wouldn't have been able to do anything.

My word didn't count. I was still his wife. My lawyer had informed me that John was trying to convince everyone that I was a "lying, revengeful bitch." Without a witness, my father's torched house and my brother's terror were invalidated. It was as if John had been given the message to proceed. He'd already gotten by with attempted murder and arson. What would he do next? How could I stop him?

The protection I'd been taught I was guaranteed as a citizen was a myth. Just as religion had lied about God, education had lied about the effectiveness of the law. What other facts had I been taught that would turn out to be propaganda?

When I got off the phone my supervisor called me into her office.

"Please sign this resignation form. It's nothing personal; your work is fine, but I think it's best you stay home. I can't have your husband disrupting the office." She smiled nervously as she handed me the pink slip.

CHAPTER 20

"Mama Said There'd Be Days Like This"

Without a job and with John stalking me, I had to take a bus down to the welfare department and apply for assistance to live on. No one would hire me. I had no experience and did not feel I could endanger any more people by my presence than I already had. As usual, I felt guilty for taking up space in the world.

I was happy to be home with Kenny again. He had frightening nightmares and his drawings were becoming morbid. He drew black, heavy bars across pages and pages of paper. He drew fires and guns and souls leaving dead bodies. John's behavior and our intolerable situation had surely created fear and emotional unrest in Kenny.

The welfare caseworker said I was eligible for a grant for business school. I received a welfare supplement of $262 a month. Out of that supplement I paid for rent, a bus card, food stamps, clothing, and necessities such as toilet paper, soap, and shampoo. When I found a full-time job, the supplement would be reduced gradually until I could survive at the poverty level on my own.

I remembered all the times I had heard people threaten to quit their jobs and live "high on welfare." I would gladly have traded places with those people.

The divorce was getting complicated. My attorney

issued divorce papers alluding to John's harassment. He included a court order restraining John from coming within a mile of me and Kenny except for approved visitation which would be decided when the domestic relations department concluded its investigation.

My attorney, against my wishes, had asked for more child support than John and I had agreed upon. He requested a lien on the house and a division of property, including the car. If John had not been dangerous I would have sought a fair settlement, but I only wanted a divorce and my independence.

John countersued. His attorneys brought up my adolescent psychiatric hospitalization. Yet I was not allowed to mention John's criminal record or incarceration in affidavits against him. I could not make my attorney understand that my affidavits were making John angrier and were endangering me and my family. But he went forward with a contempt hearing against John.

The telephone harassment continued. I had gotten an unlisted number but John somehow found out what it was. He called again, a week after I'd paid to have it changed.

On my way to and from school John continued to follow me in his car and on foot. I learned that the less I reacted, the quicker he went away, so I forced myself not to talk to him or acknowledge his presence. I constantly looked around me. Whenever I heard footsteps behind me, it filled me with terror, feeling I might be shot.

I prayed for God to protect me and keep Kenny safe. Knowing that I might die, I couldn't look to the future because I might have none.

During this time meditation gave me inner strength, allowing me to keep going even when everything appeared hopeless. Even so, I was very lonely and isolated. I felt responsible for the safety of the few friends I had who were still willing to risk being with me.

Whenever I began to lose hope and feel despondent, a friend came into my life. I had an increasing awareness that my new family was much larger than the one I'd left behind.

My friend Debbie had come from Nebraska to go to
school. Debbie had been abandoned by her boyfriend while she
was pregnant, but Debbie had managed to survive and had
brought a wonderful baby daughter into the world. They were
living with her grandmother in the suburbs. Debbie's optimism
about life rubbed off on me. She didn't let John's harassment
scare her away.

One morning on my way to the bus stop, I heard footsteps behind me. Before I could turn around, a teenager had
grabbed my arm and pushed me down against the sidewalk,
ripping my blouse and grabbing my purse. My glasses flew off
into the street and shattered. The thief ran to a car parked at the
corner and got inside. There were two other boys inside. They
drove away, burning rubber as they careened around the corner. I was stunned, but relieved that it hadn't been John. I
perceived my mugging as a blessing!

I got up, brushed myself off, picked up my broken
glasses, and walked back to the apartment. I couldn't go to
school that day. The thieves had my food stamp supply for a
month of groceries, pictures of Kenny and my mom that could
not be replaced, my security pass, and keys to my apartment.
My billfold had checks inside with my address printed on
them.

When I got back to the apartment I knocked on the
glass to get the attention of Tyrone, who was on duty at the
front desk. He opened the two doors for me. "What happened?"
When I explained, he asked, "Were they black?" I did not want
to answer my friend. White was the minority in that neighborhood.

"Damn," Tyrone swore under his breath. I took his
hand, "It's not your fault."

Tyrone was a meticulous dresser with a neat pompa-
dour haircut and a small, perfectly groomed mustache. He was
wonderful to me. He never tried to hustle me like other men in
the building had done.

Tyrone reported the mugging to the management and
told them to change the lock on my door. After making a report

to the police, I picked Kenny up from the daycare and went back to my apartment. I was awake most of the night knowing that the teenagers who had stolen my purse could easily come into the building with my card, ransack my apartment, or do whatever they wanted. Five days passed before the management changed the lock.

John watched me with binoculars. He called me on the phone several times a day. Sometimes he would hang up. Other times he would tell me what I was wearing, when I had company, and when I turned the lights on and off. He warned me that anyone who knew me was in danger. He started calling the guard desk and threatening Tyrone, saying he was going to "blow his nigger head off." I felt sick about it.

I had lost my job because of this harassment and now he was trying to get me evicted from my home. I was surprised and grateful that the management didn't turn against me the way my employer had. In fact, Tyrone and other guards had seen John in the parking lot with a pistol and a rifle. It was illegal for John, an ex-felon, to own a gun. The management signed an affidavit for me and issued their own restraining order against John, keeping him off the apartment grounds except for legal visitation times.

The contempt hearing was scheduled and rescheduled, prolonging the divorce proceedings.

I made friends with the daycare workers and the ministry students who ran the community center in the building. They invited me to work on the apartment newsletter. I was happy to be included. I had no life outside school and the nineteen-story apartment.

One morning as I stepped off the bus, John followed me on foot, yelling that he had paid someone to throw acid in my face and blind me. I walked quickly, trying to calm myself. I wouldn't give him the pleasure of showing my fear. I called to report it to the police. Two police officers came to the school, took notes, and left. It was getting to be a weekly event. As my attorney had advised, I carefully documented every incident of harassment. If he killed me, it might come in handy.

One night, as Kenny slept beside me on the sofabed, the phone rang. It was 1:00 A.M. I picked up the phone receiver. There was only the sound of dead space, no dial tone. Then I heard the sound of breaking glass. Kenny sat up. I lowered his head, warning him to stay down and get on the floor. We crawled into the bathroom where there were no windows. I told Kenny to stay there while I went back into the living room to get our clothes. There was a bullet hole in the window. We quickly dressed in the bathroom. I retrieved my purse and keys and followed Kenny as we crawled out the front door of our apartment and shut it behind us.

I stood up and pulled Kenny to me. "It's okay. It's okay." He was shaking.

"Where are we going, Mommy?" Kenny put his hand in mine. I kissed him, but said nothing.

We ran to the elevator and took it down to the lobby. I was so happy to see Tyrone on duty. He called the police. A half-hour later we made the report.

The police discovered two bullet holes in the window. They said the only way someone could have shot into the eighth floor apartment that way was with a rifle and a scope. The metal window casing had a gash. It appeared the bullet had entered diagonally, hit the inner window casing, and ricocheted back out, creating the second bullet hole.

After that, Kenny's nightmares intensified. Many nights he woke up crying and pointing outside. "I'm afraid of the crash in the window, Mommy." I never opened the drapes, even in the daylight. I felt even more trapped.

I had stopped visitation illegally. John was dangerous. How could I endanger my son? The domestic relations case worker I'd been assigned to came to my apartment and ordered me to give John visitation with Kenny. I went over every detail of John's criminal record and the harassment, trying to convince her that John was dangerous. She said it was "my word against his."

The fire, the shooting, the constant threats meant nothing. "If you do not give John visitation, the courts can take your son away and give him to John. You would not want that, would you?"

In the next few months "supervised visitation" was forced. It consisted of John, Kenny, and the caseworker going to a restaurant or the park. John was on his best behavior. He spent the hour with the social worker trying to discredit me and convince her that I was crazy and revengeful.

I was cross-examined over and over about my adolescence, even though I had had no more suicidal tendencies since leaving the Catholic Church. I had every reason to be depressed and frightened. I was not paranoid. If anything, I had under-reacted. I didn't know how to admit or express anger.

After a month of "supervised visitation," John was given visitation on alternate Sundays. I had to take Kenny to the door of the apartment at 10:00 A.M. and watch him walk out and climb into John's truck, not knowing if Kenny would be safe. He was only five years old.

Whenever Kenny returned from seeing his father, he was anxious and upset. He drew more pictures of fire, guns, black clouds, and angry faces. He had terrifying nightmares and begged me not to go anywhere without him, fearing that I would not return.

John harassed me through Kenny. Every time he came home, Kenny relayed messages to me that John had given him—"Daddy said he was going to put you in a wheel chair!" "Daddy has guns."

When I reported this emotional abuse to the authorities, the caseworker accused me of coaching Kenny to say those things. From the beginning I had gone out of my way to explain John's behavior to Kenny. I told him his daddy was hurt and sick and didn't mean to hurt us.

On one occasion John bribed Kenny into giving him my third unlisted number. Kenny cried when he told me, feeling guilty that he had given out the number. Kenny would hear John calling and threatening my family on the phone and then hear me receive a call from my frightened relatives.

Kenny was no longer a happy little boy. He often cried hysterically, throwing himself on the floor and kicking his feet until he was stiff and breathless. I sat on the floor trying to hold him. When the spells ended, I rocked him in my arms as he sobbed and gasped for air. He fell asleep exhausted, only to wake up a few hours later from a terrifying nightmare.

I felt like a bad mother, as if I could not protect my own son. I thought many times during those weeks that I would get sterilized to make sure that no other child would be born to me and have to go through what Kenny was going through.

Kenny and I had lived for over a year in constant crisis and often celebrated just being alive. There was no normal life for us. If the harassment ever ended I would have to learn how to be a "normal" parent. Kenny and I were two lone soldiers fighting a war with John and the system. We had no weapons—only the truth.

At the same time the child welfare caseworker had turned against us, my attorney began to complain that John was calling and harassing him. Mr. Benson became furious because someone had torn apart the leather seats in his Corvette. He believed my husband was responsible! He yelled at me, "Your husband is a dangerous maniac!" The detached attorney had lost his cool.

I calmly asked Mr. Benson the same questions he had been asking me for nearly a year. "Can you prove it was him? Without a witness, it's your word against his." The great attorney, Mr. Benson, hung up on me.

The next week I received a bill for over nine hundred dollars from him. In 1975 this was quite an inflated filing fee, since I was not yet divorced and had received no protection. Mr. Benson worked for Legal Aid Society and with my sister present had given me an estimate of under a hundred dollars.

I wrote a letter to the Legal Aid Society requesting a new attorney and enclosing a copy of Mr. Benson's $900 invoice.

Shortly after, I received a threatening letter from Mr. Benson filled with legalese, requesting that any further contact

I had with him be in the presence of an "adult." He had transferred my file to another attorney. He told me I had a "Jekyll
and Hyde personality" and said I was wrong to have "publi-
cized confidential information." By that he must have meant
showing his invoice to Legal Aid.

I found my own attorney, Sheldon, who retrieved my
files and took on my case.

CHAPTER 21

"I'm Still Standing"

In the Spring of 1975 I graduated from business school. My friend Debbie persuaded me to get away for awhile and drive back with her to her hometown in Nebraska. Kenny and I packed our bags and at 2 o'clock in the morning, threw them into the trunk of Debbie's car and took off, hoping to avoid John. Kenny sat in the back seat with Debbie's two-year-old, Melanie.

It was a glorious feeling of exodus to escape from the city without any sign of John. As I watched a beautiful sunrise, I wished we never had to return. When would I have my freedom?

In Nebraska we had a wonderful time visiting the old farm and sitting around the family dinner table where everyone said grace before sharing a hot meal. Debbie's family gave us a warm welcome. For the first time in months I watched Kenny play outside without him worrying about leaving my side. That night I watched him fall asleep easily and sleep soundly through the night without having one nightmare.

All too soon we had to pack up and head back to the Twin Cities.

The further away we got from Nebraska the more fidgety Kenny became. He teased Melanie and played too rough.

I turned and grabbed Kenny by the arm, "You play nice

now, Kenny. You're a lot bigger than Melanie. She's only a baby. You need to be gentle with her."

Just as I finished my lecture, Kenny started to scream, "Daddy's hurting Grandpa! Daddy's hurting Grandpa!" Debbie pulled the car over on the shoulder of the road and stopped.

As I got to the back seat blood poured out of Kenny's nose. His eyes rolled back and his body stiffened in my arms. I tried to stop the bleeding. I was frightened. First, his skin turned red and then he went white as bond paper. He was hardly breathing and I thought he was dying. I climbed inside the car and held him, rocking him in my arms.

We were in the middle of nowhere with nothing but fields of wheat for miles in all directions.

I shut the car door and asked Debbie to drive until we got to a hospital. Kenny's eyes were closed and he lay still in my arms. He was still breathing, but I didn't know what was wrong. Melanie sat quietly in the back seat watching. I only knew that Kenny was scared of going back home—where "Daddy was hurting Grandpa."

I had known from the beginning that the harassment hurt him deeply, and I had tried everything in my power to protect Kenny from John, but no one would listen. Any counselor I had talked to insisted on teaching me parenting skills, saying Kenny was too young for therapy. I had resolved to try again to get help for him. My saying no to Kenny's negative demands for attention was not going to make Kenny feel safe from John.

By the time we reached the hospital Kenny had fallen asleep in my arms. The nurse took his temperature. It was 103 degrees. The nosebleed had stopped. He had calmed down. The nurse brought him a popsicle. We stayed there for three hours until his temperature returned to normal.

The doctor released him from the hospital. "It's probably a virus," he said. "Give him plenty of liquids."

I knew when I returned home I had to find a child psychologist who could understand the damage that was being done to my little boy. I had worked for so long to rid myself of the fears in my own childhood and now before my eyes I had to witness Kenny being emotionally tortured. I felt responsible. I thought that if I had not been so screwed up as a teenager he would never have had to go through this. I would never again put another child through this hell on earth.

The week we returned, Kenny's nightmares worsened and he had an asthma attack for the first time in his life.

Family Services assigned a child psychologist to evaluate me, John, and Kenny for the custody case and make a recommendation to the court.

The psychologist spent most of the time talking to me. I had hoped he would develop a trusting relationship with Kenny alone. Kenny needed the role model of a rational and sensitive man. The therapy focused on evaluating John's and my parenting skills, rather than Kenny's response to John's behavior. I had no choice but to stick it out. Kenny's fate rested in the hands of this psychologist.

Kenny and I were ready for a move. I didn't know how I could afford another place. I needed a secure place and very low rent. It had to be near a bus line.

The lower level of my brother's old duplex became available. I decided it was just the change we needed. The crooked, pink house had green trim and leaned to the left. It was an old, drafty place with four big rooms. The neighborhood was filled with large families as poor as Kenny and I were. Kenny played outside the first day and made friends with five neighbor boys. He had so much fun that day he didn't want to come inside when it was time for bed.

Even though it was a poor neighborhood, it was wonderful. There were rows of houses, empty lots, and fields. There was a playground nearby and a friendly corner grocer only a block away. We lived on a dead-end street, with no noisy freeway running in back of us. We could hear the chatter of birds and squirrels in the trees. The old man who lived upstairs had a scrappy looking dog named Pepper with a chewed-up ear.

It was 1976 and I was hopeful. I had a different place to live and a caring attorney.

My new attorney, Sheldon, was an idealist who gave free legal services to people because he had a big heart. I was impressed with his intelligence and kindness.

Sheldon had written a manuscript about securing world peace through the legal system and let me read it. I shared my poetry with him. He liked it. I was flattered that he cared what happened to me and believed I had a worthwhile life ahead of me. He had quickly won my trust.

The psychologist's final report to the domestic relations department was in my favor. He recommended that I receive custody and described me as an intelligent and caring mother. My secret fear that I might be "crazy" was laid to rest. I could begin to heal the wounds of the past and John could no longer use the earlier misdiagnosis against me.

But the psychologist had approved limited visitation and that upset me. "After all," he said, "John is Kenny's father."

"Yes, but would you allow your children to be alone with this man?"

He thought for a moment and answered, "No."

John's harassment got more bizarre. He threw rocks in Dad's living room window. He called my brother and threatened to bomb Dad's house when we were there on Thanksgiving.

Kenny told me that John had little dolls made up to look like me and my dad. He stuck pins in them and told Kenny that he was hurting us.

I reported everything Kenny told me to the visitation worker. Despite John's odd behavior and because of the psychologist's recommendation about visitation, she refused to monitor his visitation. He had been harassing us for two years.

One night I was at my father's doing laundry. I had a tape recorder ready near the phone to record John's next call. When the phone rang I answered it and signaled to Dad that it was John.

Dad went upstairs to the second phone to listen. John began his usual tirade.

"You cocksucker. Your brothers are a bunch of faggots! I'm going to kill your whole fucking family and finish the job this time!"

He was in a particularly foul mood and I hadn't said a word to provoke him. When he hung up I rewound the tape and played it back. I had become numb to his crude threats after hearing them for so long. Sweet God, I finally had his threats on tape.

John was due to pick Kenny up at Dad's house in less than thirty minutes for his approved visitation.

I ran up the steps with the recorder to tell Dad the good news. He wasn't in the bedroom where the phone was. The bathroom door was open. I heard water running.

I went in and saw Dad leaning against the sink quickly putting two nitroglycerine tablets in his mouth.

"Are you okay?" I put my hand on his back.

"My chest is tightening up!" His voice was shaky. "I'll be all right. I just have to sit down." He put down the toilet seat cover and sat down to rest on the stool. I was scared and hurt at the same time.

I realized then it was the first time Dad really believed how dangerous John was. Maybe now he could understand how tormented I had felt each time I sent Kenny out the door with John because of "the law." Law and justice were not synonymous.

Half an hour later Dad and I waited in the living room wondering if John would show up.

Sure enough, he drove his pickup to the curb, parked, and walked nonchalantly up to the house, whistling. John had always played the "good guy" in front of my father. He obviously didn't realize that Dad had heard his threats on the other phone.

Dad went towards the door.

"Are you sure you feel up to this?" I was afraid Dad would have a heart attack.

He didn't answer me.

John knocked.

Leaving the chain on, Dad opened the door.

John smiled. "I'm here for Kenny."

"*I* was on that phone. I heard everything." Then Dad shouted, "Get off my property! You're trespassing!"

"Give me Kenny!" John said. "I got my rights!"

Dad shut the door in John's face and backed away with his hand on his chest. "It's okay. Just tight...no pain. I think I'd better lie down." He slowly went up the stairs to his bedroom.

"Do you want me to call an ambulance, Dad?"

"No, no. I'll be okay," he said as he reached the landing.

"Thanks, Dad. Thanks!"

The week of the first contempt hearing I had seven witnesses present to testify. The evidence against John was finally going to be heard.

When John's attorney came out of the courtroom and saw my witnesses, his mouth dropped open and his face turned bright red. He excused himself and went back into the chambers.

A few minutes later he came out and went to the elevator. We were informed by the clerk of court that John's attorney had had a gallbladder attack and the hearing was postponed— for the third time.

CHAPTER 22

"I Am A Rock"

By the time the hearing came up on the court agenda
again, half the witnesses I had the first time were unavailable.
It was not long into the hearing that it became obvious the
judge had chosen to believe John's lies rather than the documented evidence of harassment in affidavits and police reports.
He gave a long lecture about the law and told my brothers,
"Stop acting as a posse and taking the law into your own
hands!"

Ironically, my brothers had been extremely tolerant. No
one was more peaceful and nonviolent than my brothers. They
had never retaliated, despite John's death threats. Once again,
the victims were being admonished. Terry, who had survived
the fire, listened to this judge give orders based on John's lies.

We patiently waited for it to end. The judge did warn
that harassment would not be tolerated on either side. When the
hearing was over I felt no safer than I had before. He had given
us no hope for protection.

The harassment continued. One week I arranged with
the visitation case worker to change a Sunday of John's visitation so Kenny could go with me to an out-of-town wedding.
John and I had both received a letter approving this change.

That weekend my sister and her husband Ray picked us

up and we headed for Wisconsin. After the wedding we stayed at a nearby motel. Later, Ray heard something in the parking lot. When he looked out he saw John's car on the road.

Before we left town we stopped for gas. When Ray took off the gas cap he saw that the rim of the gas tank was coated with sugar. If he had driven the car any further, the sugar would have ruined the engine.

Ray and friends we knew in town spent the day cleaning the sugar out of the gas tank and fuel lines.

When we finally arrived back in the Cities, we stopped at Dad's house. Dad informed me that the visitation case worker had called several times and was upset because John had obtained her unlisted number and harassed her.

She called again and screamed at me. Her usual calm manner had disappeared. "Did you give John my phone number? He's been calling my home and harassing me."

I couldn't believe what I heard. Like my former attorney, she couldn't handle the slightest interference in *her* life, but had accused me of overreacting to arson, shooting, and endless violence.

"Listen, I don't know your phone number. Okay? John is angry because you approved the visitation change for the weekend. I had to change my number three times. I don't know what else you can do."

"He has to be stopped." The woman was adamant.

"I've been telling you for two years what he's been doing to Kenny and me. I'm sorry he's bothering you. John followed us to Wisconsin and tampered with my brother-in-law's car. All you can do is report it. He'll lie his way out of it the way he always does."

She started to cry on the phone. "I'm pregnant. I can't have him harassing me like this."

"How do you think I feel every time I send Kenny out the door with him because of your rules? Maybe when you have a child you'll understand. I have to go report the car tampering to the police."

There was silence on the other end of the line. How

ironic that she wanted me to make her feel better. I never talked to her again. She went on maternity leave and transferred my file to a new case worker.

The harassment escalated as Thanksgiving approached. John threatened to bomb Dad's house. My family came together and took the tape recorded threats to the county attorney, requesting protection and enforcement of the restraining order. The county attorney politely declined our request. He had the power to put a warrant out for John's arrest for contempt of court. He refused.

The next week when Kenny and I went out into the hallway of our duplex, there was a slaughtered muskrat in the front of our door. This did not look like an animal that had been found in the street. It was newly-killed. It had been sawed down the middle and left with the bloody entrails hanging out. John's words echoed in my head, "You're next!"

Kenny told me he had seen the tail of an animal sticking out of a bag in the back seat of John's car.

After the voodoo dolls and the slaughtered animal, I went to the mental health department for help.

I waited in the lobby while the social worker investigated John's prison record, checking his mental status during his incarceration. He came back shaking his head and called me into his office.

"Stillwater Prison referred me back to St. Peter's, a security prison hospital for the criminally insane. Your husband was there for several years. He was diagnosed as a sociopath and considered dangerous by the prison staff."

"Can he be committed for treatment?" I thought I was finally going to get help.

"John is a sociopath." The man explained, "Sociopaths

are considered incurable, therefore, commitment is a waste of our time. Even if we could do something, John would be released in seventy-two hours angrier than before."

Having exhausted the legal and social resources, I went to a battered women's shelter for advice. I recounted the long, sordid story. The advocate told me they had a wonderful attorney, an expert in abuse who could possibly help me. She wrote his name on a piece of paper. Mr. Benson. My first attorney! I began to feel as if this was a dream. How could this be happening?

From there, I went to a walk-in crisis center and told the whole story all over again. The volunteer informed me that the center knew a wonderful judge and suggested I have my attorney arrange a hearing in front of this judge. His name— Judge Saunders, the same judge who had accused my brothers of being a posse.

I left the crisis center weary of trying to protect myself and Kenny. If John was determined to murder us, so be it. It was out of my control. Our fate lay in God's hands. I had done everything humanly possible to defend myself within the law.

After graduating from business school I applied for several secretarial positions and waited to get a phone call for an interview. I prayed I would get a job before John found out my fourth unlisted number. I wanted to be totally independent of the welfare system.

Sunday afternoon the phone rang. John was on the line repeating his obscene threats. I set the phone down on my bed and let him threaten the pillow.

Kenny played outside. I locked the door and left the house. We walked to the corner store and used the pay phone. I called the phone company. I couldn't get my number changed until Monday.

I called Dad and asked if I could get a ride over to his place to do some laundry. I didn't want to talk about the harassment. We were all tired of it.

As I sorted clothes in the basement I had to hold back my tears. I went upstairs and asked Dad to watch Kenny for me while I went to the store to buy bleach. I was out the door before he had answered me. I had to get away.

It was dark outside. I felt like a zombie, too numb to be afraid. I walked over the hill, taking a shortcut I had taken as a child. I was a block away from the store when John drove by and shouted threats out of the open window.

An intense rage rose in my throat. I would not let him intimidate me anymore. At that moment I saw in front of me on the grass a large rock the size of a football. Engulfed by a feeling of peace, and without hesitation, I picked up the stone and hid it under my jacket. I waited for John to come back, as I knew he would.

According to the latest restraining order, John was ordered not to be within a mile radius of me, except for visitation, which was a week away.

Sure enough, as I neared the corner, John drove by yelling obscenities. I raised the stone. With all my strength I threw the rock into the window behind John's head. His mouth dropped open as shattered glass flew around him.

A feeling of triumph filled me, releasing the fear in my heart. A man walking across the street stared in disbelief. John drove away.

I walked into the store, still shaking and bought a jug of bleach, expecting the police to rush in at any moment and arrest me. The man who'd seen me throw the rock into John's car came into the store and stared at me until I left.

I walked back to Dad's house feeling pleased. I had finally stood up for myself. If John did go to the police he'd have to explain what he was doing driving by me on a non-visitation day, against the restraining order.

When I got in the door I hugged Kenny as hard as I could. Dad asked me if I felt better after taking a walk.

"Yes," I said, "much better!"

Two weeks later I received a subpoena to appear in court on charges of criminal assault. The order was signed by the county attorney who a few weeks earlier had refused to put a warrant out for John's arrest.

CHAPTER 23

"Killing Me Softly"

John never followed me again.

Nine months later I appeared in court for the criminal assault charges against me. John didn't show up. Sheldon convinced the judge that my action had been self-defense. The charges were dropped.

My divorce finally went through.

It was a struggle for Kenny and me to learn to live without crisis and to trust again. We were still poor, buying secondhand clothes and riding the bus. But we were filled with the joy of living without fear.

No longer would I let fear run my life. My fear of a punishing God had guided so much of my earlier life and taken my power away. That left me vulnerable to the abuses of the mental health profession, to the inequality of the legal system, and finally to the dangers of an out-of-control ex-husband. My experiences began to teach me that I was safe despite the external "dangers" of the world.

Beliefs are a magnet and draw to you what you believe. It's the reality of "ask and you shall receive." If you believe suffering is good you will receive suffering, as my mother had. The Universe does not judge; it gives what you ask. If you believe in doom and gloom, they are yours for the having.

When I stopped believing in a distant, rigid, and egotistical God and accepted an intimate, accepting, and loving God, good things began to come to me.

One evening, after the divorce, I received a call from Michael, my long-lost boyfriend. He was dying of leukemia. The doctor had told him he had two weeks to live, so he contacted people from his past.

When Michael first learned about the cancer he had two young boys and his beautiful wife was pregnant with their third child. He fought hard and hung on. He lived three more years. Michael underwent chemotherapy with experimental drugs and survived to see the birth of his daughter.

When I visited him in the hospital I had to wear a gown, mask, and gloves. As I peeked around the door I had expected to see a sickly, dying man. Except for having no hair, Michael looked very much the way he had when we were dating. In that short time in his hospital room we shared the events we had lived through since Michael had been drafted and had left on the train for boot camp. We were still friends, as though no time had gone by.

The greatest part of seeing Michael was knowing that he had forgiven me for not waiting for him. We had lost the infatuation of youth and were meant to live our lives apart. Our first love had taught us we could love. Life had taught us that love changes, but never dies. When I left, I thanked him for letting me say good-bye this time.

Nine months later, at midnight, the ringing phone woke me up. Michael was on the line. He told me his legs were full of holes from shots of morphine and he was in pain. He drifted in and out of consciousness. One minute he was asking about Kenny and my job and the next he was hallucinating. I don't know how he had managed to remember my phone number. Michael said he was "goin' fishin." That was how Michael referred to dying.

"Save some fish for me, Michael." I tried not to fall apart on the phone.

After fifteen minutes of scattered conversation, Michael fell asleep. I rested the receiver next to my ear and listened to his breathing. Too soon, I heard someone come into his hospital room and hang up the receiver. I knew I would never talk to Michael again—in this life.

His sister called me two days later. Michael had passed on.

When I finally stood up for myself and threw that rock at John, I understood on a deeper level that I was responsible for what happened to me. I had learned not to waste time worrying about what I had no control over, however unjust. My background had taught me to trust authority without discernment and experts without wisdom. It had taught me it was wrong to use the mind God had given me.

In a different time one might live an entire life without being harmed by believing without question everything one was taught. What was true in the forties and fifties didn't work in the sixties and seventies.

John's mixed messages and emotional abuse had robbed my son of a childhood. His behavior had harassed me out of a job.

But the rock was John's language. He had never understood my language. The rock said, "You can't do this to me anymore!" John's behavior changed immediately.

I was finally hired as a receptionist. The harassment calls stopped.

In an effort to get off assistance I changed jobs often, taking a better paying job whenever I could. Each time I received a raise, my supplement was cut until I was able to survive at the poverty level on my own.

Happiness is relative. I never felt more blessed. It was wonderful to answer the phone knowing that no one was on the line cursing and threatening my life. It took me another year to accept that I wasn't going to be shot in the back on the way to the bus. Kenny and I had lived each day prepared for separation and death. After living in crisis we had to learn to live a normal life.

I had to be realistic about what I could achieve as a single parent with some clerical skills and no college degree. I gave up the idea of owning a house or even a car.

To the world I was a nothing. I had received welfare. I was a divorcee who lived in a dumpy duplex, wore secondhand clothes, and took the bus. In the seventies, by American standards, I should have had a degree, a career, a man, a mortgage and house in the suburbs, a family plan, a retirement plan, and a funeral plot.

But I was a survivor. I was free. I had my mental and physical health, my integrity, and my honesty. I was strong, independent. I was no longer a victim! I loved my son, my God, and myself. No one could take my new beliefs away from me. And I wanted to live!

No church, no judge, no welfare worker, no employer, no man would ever make me hate myself again.

I knew I could stand alone in God. I had learned that even without a man or without a child, I was somebody.

I believe in God, who never abandoned me.

For me, changing my beliefs and getting strong, was not a "born again" experience. It was the process of life unfolding before me like a rolled-out carpet. How fast I chose to walk up that carpet was up to me. I had free will.

If I learned anything, it was that nothing but God is absolute. It was not one person, event, or practice that changed my life. All people have their own timing and their own path. We may all be moving toward the same end, but I cannot honestly judge where others are on their path. I don't know where they came from or where they are going. I have known Christlike people of every religion. Sheldon, the Jewish attorney who helped me, was more Christlike than the many Christians I had encountered.

It took me many years of purging my feelings, writing and rewriting, to forgive the Catholic Church. Many people I love and respect are Catholic. They tell me the Church has changed. It doesn't matter. I cannot belong to a church that does not represent my faith. Nor have I found comfort in other religions.

Most religions treat women as spiritually inferior to men. God is Spirit. We are Spirit. The physical body we are born into has nothing to do with our worth! When women stop participating in religions that see them as inferior, religions will lose their power.

False religions would die tomorrow if women took their children's hands and walked out of church.

When the harassment ended, my life was still a struggle. I had things to work out. I had to learn to trust again. I had to learn the politics of business. I had to learn to leave men who didn't accept me for who I was.

Not only was I given loving friends when I needed them, I was given other ways of healing including meditation, therapy, metaphysics, hypnosis, alternative medicine, and counseling. Often, it was the integrity and love of the teacher that helped me as much as what was being taught.

In the seventies I met a gifted psychic named David. When there was no future in sight for me, David saw a vision of a life ahead for me. He saw me happily married, when no one loved me. He saw me as a published author, when I wasn't writing. And he referred me to a progressive counselor named June.

June helped me become more objective about the abuse I'd lived through. She helped me to focus on the present and the future, not on the past.

She saw my potential. The most powerful gift June gave me was a hug every time I saw her. She validated my existence.

She was the mother I had lost. She was the role model of a woman who had survived a divorce herself and started a new career in mid-life.

June saw the world as it was. She didn't hide behind ideology or authority. She helped me face the grieving child inside. My inability to deal with anger had kept me a victim longer than necessary. Accepting my anger, letting go of denial, was the only way I could free myself from the past and behave as an adult, responsible for my own destiny.

June understood the psychiatric abuse I'd been through. She admitted there was abuse within the therapeutic community. I paid June fifteen dollars an hour. In her modest office a disturbed child became a healthy adult.

There were some painful sessions with June when she confronted me with my denial. I wanted to quit, but I went back. And that's when I truly began to heal.

With June, I was finally able to forgive the psychiatric abuse and let go of it.

And she gave me a most amazing gift. She told me I no longer required her services, that I was capable of coping on my own. She let me go—without a label.

I was not happy the day she told me this. I felt that I'd lost my best friend. I grieved that relationship for a long time. She was one of the many people who appeared in my life when I needed a lifeline.

I wanted to share my life again. I wanted the warmth of a man holding me in the night. This time I wasn't looking for a father for myself or my child.

I didn't want to be supported financially or to have to obey a man again the way I had obeyed John. I knew if I played the game of servant to get a husband I'd be serving for the rest of my life. I was not about to replace a man's mother.

Anyone who wanted me had to accept where I'd been and where I was going.

I dated quite often and fell in love too easily, often choosing "commitment phobics." I was often hurt, but never quit hoping. I wrote the pain out of my heart by journaling.

David, the psychic, once told me that I believed I

couldn't have my writing and a good man, too. He said when I changed that belief, I would have both. I already knew that changing my beliefs changed my reality. I began to project a new reality—I deserved unlimited love and unlimited success.

CHAPTER 24

"Could I Have This Dance For the Rest Of My Life?"

On Halloween, 1981, my friend Bonnie insisted I go to a giant costume party sponsored by WWTC Radio. The event took place at Castle Royale, a new restaurant built in the underground caves in the bluffs above the Mississippi River in St. Paul.

I didn't want to go. I was trying to forget the end of a recent relationship. I had met the last man I'd dated on the rebound. I didn't need to meet another man right now. But Bonnie was a close friend and I was easily persuaded.

In Coon Rapids, a suburb of Minneapolis, William Gorden Michael had planned to go duck hunting. His friend Ray had persuaded him to stay home Saturday night and go to the Halloween bash. Duck hunting could wait until next week. He didn't want to go. He hadn't recovered from his year-old divorce. But Ray was his close friend and Bill was easily persuaded.

I had planned to wear a plastic terrarium on my head and go as a Martian, but I couldn't figure out what to wear for the spacesuit. Instead, I went down to the Salvation Army and found an old fashioned dress. I decorated a wide-brimmed straw hat with flowers and went as a Victorian lady. Bonnie dressed as a gypsy.

The restaurant, a combination bar and dance floor, extended into several chambers in the caves. We each bought a beer and wandered through the caves circling the rooms, watching people arrive in elaborate costumes, wondering who would win the contest for best costume. The radio station broadcasted from the caves that night and music thundered inside, bouncing off the sandstone walls.

After our second drink, Bonnie and I started to converse with monsters, bees, vampires, and men wearing dresses with water-balloon boobs. As the night wore on, the place grew livelier and more crowded. At around eleven, the music stopped and the contest began. People crowded around the stage to get a closer look at the best costumes.

Bonnie and I left the crowded, smoky room and stopped at the bar. Ray started to talk to Bonnie. He turned to me and said his buddy Bill had gone outside.

I stood at the bar looking around the crowd. I spotted him in the doorway, dressed as a farmer. That must be Bill, I thought. He was tall, with brown hair, a heavy, dark beard and blue eyes. He wore a white T-shirt and a red kerchief around his neck. He looked irritated.

He walked over to the bar and offered to buy me a drink.

"I'll just have a Coke, thanks. I've already had too many."

He bought me a pop. I thanked him and asked him if he was married.

"No, divorced," he said and looked over at Ray and Bonnie. Then he looked back at me as if seeing me for the first time. Bill said he had already left the party and gone out to his truck to wait for Ray to come out so they could go home. But Ray never came out and Bill knew that if Ray started talking to someone he'd never leave. Tired of waiting, Bill came back into the party to search for his buddy.

By the time the contest ended, Bill and I were dancing. After the last dance he walked with me to the car and asked for my phone number. I could not find a pen in my purse so I scribbled my unlisted number on a scrap of paper in eyebrow pencil. I didn't expect him to call me.

Here was this tall, dark, and handsome man. (Bill would like me to keep this in the book.) And I kept affirming, "I deserve a loving, permanent relationship!"

Bill did call. I remember the day. Kenny had come in from outside crying because someone had stolen his bicycle. I had to ask Bill to call back because I had to deal with the crisis. I was sure that Bill, being a very eligible man, was not going to be thrilled with my domestic problems of childrearing. It was not a romantic way to start out. Most men I had dated took some time to warm up to a child or never did at all and only dated me on the weekends Kenny was gone, which was a sign there was no future in that particular relationship. I wondered if Bill would even call back.

But to my surprise he did. Bill confesses now that he had once had a rule not to date women with children. But he eased the rule to let one eleven-year-old boy into his life.

Kenny did not make it easy. He had survived a domestic war and anyone who wanted his mother would have to meet the test.

I feared Bill getting close to Kenny and then leaving us. Kenny did not need any more abandonment than he had already experienced. Bill, too, was vulnerable from his divorce.

That first year we behaved much like teenagers, lovemaking, fighting, breaking up, and reuniting. But we fell in love.

Slowly we accomplished a hard-won trust among the three of us. Kenny began to call Bill "Dad." Then Kenny announced he now wished to be called "Ken." My "baby" was growing up.

We weathered the most difficult adjustments and on October 6, 1984, we were married.

I have learned to trust and depend on Bill. It feels sweet, warm, and safe.

It is now Saturday afternoon. The morning thunderstorm has passed through and it has turned into a beautiful day. Bill is barbecuing chicken on the grill and we are going to eat in the back yard at the picnic table. We have a wonderful back yard with many giant pines by the fence. Because railroad tracks run behind our house we have no neighbors there and lots of privacy.

The most beautiful tree in the yard is the largest maple I have ever seen. Not far in front of the bay window Bill installed recently in the kitchen is a birch tree his dog Flicka likes to sit under and watch for birds who dare land in her territory. She is the great protector of our yard.

There is a gentle breeze sweeping through the trees and God is outside whispering—like the air, free, quiet, limitless, and always here.

"Imagine...No Religion"

Sunday, May 9, 1993

It is Mother's Day, an appropriate day I thought to sit out on the front porch that Bill was building in the first chapter of *Vows of Silence* and update the final chapter again. You see, it was ten years ago that Bill built this front porch and I started to write the first version of *Vows of Silence*. I must tell you what has happened since then. It has taken me ten years to find a publisher.

Bill is grieving his closest friend, his Lady Flicka. She had to be put to sleep last January. The back yard even misses its protector. The birds and rabbits venture closer to the house now.

Ken is a twenty-three-year-old man. He has beautiful blue-green eyes and thick, curly hair. Girls frequently fall in love with him and he runs away from them. His mother sides with the girls, remembering the pain of rejection.

Ken moved out of the house more than a year ago. Despite my writing and all my intentions of not going through "empty nest syndrome," grieving hit hard. I have spent a good portion of these last ten years letting go of the pain and anger of the past. I have grieved the death of my brother David, who died of a massive coronary at age forty-seven. I went to a grief counselor to find out how to fill the holes in my heart. In that process, I realized that during the ten years I had written and rewritten *Vows of Silence*, I had been actively grieving my mother and her silences through my writing.

With all the truth that is coming to the surface in this decade such as incest, rape, child abuse, political corruption, and sexual harassment, there appears to be a spiritual evolution that has brought us to a point in human history where our desire for truth will no longer support denial and oppression. Although it appears that the world is crumbling, miracles are occurring every day. The raised consciousness of the world is like a giant searchlight scanning every corner of the earth and exposing any hypocrisy. The Universe is supporting the truth, and any structure built on deceit, ego, or greed is crumbling. The meek are inheriting the earth and anyone with evil intent will not escape the scrutiny of the light. Every prayer for peace is contributing to this miracle.

I have learned that people can and do change when they make the choice to do that—sometimes people I least expected.

In 1991, during the war in Saudi Arabia, I stopped in the atrium of the Minneapolis Government Center to hear the speakers at a peace rally during lunch.

The second speaker was conservatively dressed in a suit and tie. He said he was an attorney, a member of the Veterans Against the War, and spoke honestly about teaching guerrilla warfare in Vietnam. He openly described seeing Vietnamese orphans find their parents' mutilated bodies. He shared the grief of losing his own troops. It was the memory of a soldier, a friend he had watched die that had driven him to the podium that day. The winter sun streamed through the two-story windows illuminating the space. I felt I had entered a dream as I recognized the face of the man who talked into the microphone ten feet from me.

The courageous man speaking was my first divorce attorney, Mr. Benson, whom I had been angry with for not protecting me and Kenny.

He was now, ironically, protecting my son with his stance against the war. Ken was ripe to be drafted if war in the Middle East had gone on much longer.

When the rally ended I summoned the boldness to walk over to Mr. Benson and speak with him. I realized after many years that my case had not been unusual. At the end of every year, Minnesota commemorates the women and children who are killed by angry spouses and boyfriends. Last year there were thirty-eight women and six children, none of them ever mentioned on the news.

My divorce had started twenty years before and little had changed. I understood that Mr. Benson was not responsible for not protecting me.

I told him how much I admired him for coming forward to speak against the war.

"You're the one whose husband shot in your apartment window." His stern expression softened when I told him I was sorry for blaming him for not protecting me. We were both veterans, of different wars. I gave him a hug and walked away, promising myself to always see the possibility of change in everyone. I wondered what heart-opening experience had changed this man from a macho soldier ready to fight at all costs, to a peace loving, gentle spokesperson for all of our children.

People sometimes ask me what happened to Robert, the murderer. He is still in prison for the murder of Susan Marek.

He did call me from prison in 1981. I was sitting in my living room apartment folding socks when the phone rang.

"Hi," a friendly voice said. "It's Robert."

"Robert who?" I asked as I tossed a folded ball of paired socks into a pile on the sofa.

"Petraszewski," he said.

After catching my breath I asked, "How did you get my number?" It was still unlisted.

"I told your brother I was arranging a high school reunion."

The last time I had heard about Robert was when the *St. Paul Pioneer Press* ran an editorial that lambasted the penal system for allowing Robert, a heinous murderer to marry a social worker. That editorial had made me feel better. Susan and I had not been the only people fooled by this charismatic man.

"I thought you were married," I asked.

Robert told me he was now divorced. He said he had saved the essay I'd written that was published in the *Pioneer Press*. He asked if I'd visit him in prison. He was living in a minimum security cottage. I told him that I was getting married and moving out of state.

The conversation had all been very casual, but when I hung up the phone I lay down and cried. And then I immediately changed my phone number. I had learned my lesson. He sent me a card. I returned it, telling him I had forgiven him for leaving me when I was pregnant. I had no judgment about the murder. That was between him and God and the soul of Susan Marek.

My soul's search has released me from the survival guilt of Susan Marek's death. I had tried to leave this life, but was given a choice to return to give hope to others, as hope had been given to me.

There was another person from my past I gave a great big hug to when I met him—that was Steve Allen.

In 1988, I called the phone number on the stationery of the last letter I had received from Steve Allen which had been in 1974.

To my surprise his office number was the same. I wrote him a letter, but never received an answer. In 1989, I went to the Renaissance Festival and had a reading with a psychic named LaJeanne. She did not know me, but she told me that she saw me getting a book published and she saw me giving her an autographed copy. I was amazed. But why would I give this woman a copy of my book? I was excited that she saw it published. After six years of rejections, I was ready to burn the manuscript and give up.

She advised me to write Steve Allen again and something wonderful would happen.

"But I wrote him last year and he never answered!" I didn't believe her. She explained they had lost my address and I should try again.

Expecting her prediction to be a long shot, I not only copied and mailed a letter and manuscript, I asked him to write the foreword for *Vows*, figuring I had nothing to lose.

Three weeks later I received a letter from a member of Steve Allen's staff informing me that Steve had read the first three chapters and sent the manuscript to one of his publishers. He also agreed to write the foreword. He was traveling at the time and would write to me at a later date. I also learned that Steve had answered my letter of 1988, but my address had only been typed on the envelope and it had gotton lost.

LaJeanne was right.

Steve sent me more of his books. He told me he had published thirty-four books and was working on two more. I had the first fifteen books Steve had written. I went to the library to find the books I had missed. When I was running for my life, I had lost touch with Steve Allen's writing. In my scrapbook, I wrote...14 YEARS LATER: My correspondence with Steve Allen continued as though it had never stopped.

At the library I found *Beloved Son: A Story About Jesus Cults*. Steve Allen had written about his son Brian's life in a Jesus cult. No wonder he had been receptive to my book. Religion had stolen from both of us. He had lost his son to religious abuse, much as I had lost my mother. I also realized that he and I had more in common than just my fan admiration.

August
Eighth
1 9 8 9

Dear Diana:

You must have wondered if I had dropped off the end of the earth since it's been such a long time between letters.

Actually, I've been to almost every part of the country in recent weeks, doing concerts and promoting my latest book.

Enclosed is a copy of it to add to your library.

In answer to your questions about my son Brian -- his cult group, luckily, fell apart several years ago. Brian and most of the other members moved out at that time, having finally come to realize that their leader was a phony and con-man.

Congratulations again on the great progress you've made. It's always a pleasure to exchange thoughts with you.

Cordially,

Steve Allen

In August, 1990, I read an announcement in the newspaper that Roselyn Carter was scheduled to lecture at an upcoming Senior Citizens Expo. At the very bottom of the advertisement in small print was a list of other Expo guests. Steve Allen was one of them.

Suddenly meeting him mattered more than anything. I had tried to meet him twenty-seven years earlier. It was 1963 and he was master of ceremonies for the St. Paul Winter Carnival.

He broadcast his television show from the downtown St. Paul Auditorium. I sneaked backstage and waited, missing the entire show. I thought I could meet him simply because I loved him, forgetting that the ten thousand people screaming and waving behind the curtains loved him, too. When he came backstage he was surrounded by police and security guards. I chased them down the steps and out to a waiting limousine and stood in the snowbank crying as the car moved out of sight down the frozen street. I vowed that I would meet him someday.

Now that I knew he was coming to St. Paul again I called his office and arranged to see him.

Twenty-seven years after I had chased after Steve Allen at the St. Paul Winter Carnival and stood crying in the snow, I was going to meet my mentor.

I wanted to give him something besides a thank you, something tangible. But what do you give a millionaire?

One day the Universe answered my dilemma. I'd give him a crystal piano. But I'd never seen one anywhere. I checked shop after shop. They had crystal animals and odd objects, but no pianos. Two days before his arrival I was in downtown Minneapolis in the IDS Crystal Court and decided to check the Scarlet Letters gift shop one more time. In the corner of this crowded shop was a glass case filled with tiny crystal figurines. For the umpteenth time I held my breath and waited as the shelves revolved, searching for a piano. There it was! It was hiding behind a clown and a mouse—a tiny crystal grand piano, just as I had envisioned. I had learned that when you ask, it is not necessary to know where or when or how, but only to wait and be open to receive.

September 15 finally came. I could hardly wait for the concert to be over. When it ended Bill and I were led back-stage. A television crew waited to interview Steve, but a harried man came over and told us that the reporter hadn't arrived yet, so we could go next. The man opened the door and said, "Steve?"

"Yes?" A familiar voice answered as we walked down a poorly lit corridor to a small concrete room flooded in light. Steve was sitting alone in a chair. He stood. "Where do you want me?" he asked. Steve must have thought Bill was the photographer because of the camera around Bill's neck.

I said, "No, I'm Diana...." My arms shook at my sides and I blushed, afraid he was going to say, "Diana Who?"

He graciously said, "Let me give you a hug!" and Bill took the only photograph I have ever liked of myself.

The three of us talked for twenty minutes. He told us about his thirty-fourth book going to press that week—*Steve*

Allen on the Bible, Religion and Morality. He kept staring at my husband Bill and finally told us that Bill looked very much like his son David. His beard and even his glasses were the same. I remember vividly how beautiful Steve Allen's hands were. When I gave him the gift he thanked me and graciously held up the piano for Bill to take another picture. He said he knew just where he would put it, that he and Jayne had a collection of crystal.

The lighting man for the news crew knocked on the door and came in to set up for the interview. We were going to leave then, but Steve said we didn't have to go just yet. He put the piano back in its box and put it into a worn container filled with papers that had been sitting on the coffee table.

Steve stood to greet the people crowding into the small room. I handed him an envelope and asked him to read its contents later. He slipped it into the pocket of his suit coat. It was a poem I had written that morning—a poem about a sad fourteen-year-old girl and a man who had made her laugh.

When it was time to go, Bill shook his hand first. Steve held his hand out to me, but I put my arms around him again. After all, my affirmation had taken twenty-seven years to manifest. Steve hugged me back. The crew shuffled their feet nervously as we turned to leave. "Send me the picture," I heard him say as we headed down the hall. We turned back and waved, "We will, thank you!"

Whenever I look at the photo of Steve Allen and me I remember this: in their own time dreams are realized. It had been one of those perfect summer nights, when you are in the right place, at the right time, when souls come full circle and reunite.

A few weeks ago my publisher received the foreword for *Vows of Silence* from Steve Allen.

Whenever I was about to give up on this book, when the rejections became too cruel and my motivation was waning, some beautiful person, like an appearing angel, would come along and lift me up again and keep me going.

Many of those friends are visionaries, psychics who gave me hope. When John was on his rampage of violence they saw into the future, reminding me to hold on, that I would one day be married to a wonderful man.

When no one would look at my book, they saw *Vows of Silence* being published in the future, ten years before I had written a word of it.

Spiritual visionaries (not all are spiritual) are gifted by God to see into other realms and help us see beyond today's petty worries.

My experiences are too numerous and miraculous to name here in this book, but metaphysics (beyond the physical) has been a great enhancement to my spirituality. Everyone on earth is on a spiritual journey of the soul. Some do it with their eyes shut. Seekers, conscious of the journey, choose to do it with their eyes open.

I am beginning to see that the qualities of tenacious persistence with which I have pursued this book probably came from my father's influence. He is eighty-three years old and taking French and piano lessons. He practices Tai Chi and uses an exercycle and treadmill and is healthier than I am.

He is editor of the 3M Retirement Newsletter and an impressive photographer. Even though he lost his second wife Marie to cancer three years ago, he is still a vibrant, positive person, following his joy with humility and quiet faith.

I am only beginning to fully appreciate him out of the shadow of my mother.

In my search for myself, through my mother, I met my middle-namesake, Sister Louise. She admitted to me that Mother cried when she left the convent saying, "Why do you get to stay when I can't?" I had been told by the convent that Mom left because of her health and because of the undue stress she was under. How, then, did she survive the stress of raising five children? I will never know why she was forced out of the convent. It was her priest advisor's decision, not hers. Was she a "temptation" to a doctor or a priest?

I have been told by former nuns that nursing orders take care of their own when they are sick; they do not kick them out of the convent.

Dad admitted to me he was in love with Mom in high school, but she had been determined to be a nurse and to follow her "divine calling." Dad drove her to the convent the day she entered. Her mother rode in the car with them and chastised Dad for not marrying Mom. "You could have stopped her!" she told him on the way back home to Chippewa Falls, Wisconsin.

Dad and I both knew my mother was too stubborn to let anyone influence her decision, particularly if she believed it was a divine calling.

When I was helping Dad discard some belongings recently, I discovered an essay my mother had written in 1954 describing how she was not able to reconcile her spiritual experience with her religious indoctrination.

> *When I left the convent about fifteen years ago, I could only feel a great wound. It was such that neither bitterness, disillusionment, anxiety, nor the supposed humiliation of it could replace the one question. Why must this happen to me?*
>
> *I knew in my soul that I had tried to live the religious life as such, in far more intense measure than many of my co-sisters and yet it was, as it were, suffocating the very things I had been seeking. I did not try to answer the question then, nor had I any desire to do so in the near future. I was too tired, so very tired that even death would have been easier to face than the readjustment to a new life....*

Next she began to describe prophetically my own journey. It looked hauntingly like my own writing:

> *I had to go on. My faith was still there, my desires for contemplation were just as urgent; but I have kept them dormant and subdued all these years, for I never wanted to be drawn again into things I would never understand.*

But there the similarities end. She went on to describe her loyalty:

I am a firm believer in the basic doctrines of the Catholic Church, one who cares enough about her creed to point out its immaturities as well as its life-giving and God-given holiness.

Adelaide Ann Findlay-LeMay (Sister Mary Lucy)

I have been accused of losing my faith, but I can honestly thank the Roman Catholic Church now. It is like my first marriage. Had the Church not been so damaging in the first place, like John, I might never have left. I might never have found the joy and healing I now have in my spiritual life. I might never have released the guilt and loved myself, might never have allowed the good to come into my life.

What do I believe in without a church?

Besides surviving a fatal suicide attempt and witnessing the events in this story, I have seen too many things happen that are beyond coincidence that show God manifest everywhere in life, not trapped in false idols and narrow dogma.

I know that some theologians, scientists, and intellectuals will invalidate my life and other people's truth as "anecdotal" and stay stuck in their superiority, denial, and fear, but others will feel less alone because they have come to know the same renewing truth of God.

I am not my body. I am an eternal divine spirit without beginning or end. Death is an illusion. We are either in a body or out of a body. I no longer fear punishment or suffer from the beliefs that once caused so much pain.

I have forgiven my abusers and I would not punish anyone with eternal damnation. Can God be less loving and forgiving than I? There is no hell but the suffering humans have created by using free will to create the lie that we are separate from God. Humanity created suffering, not God. But we can change our beliefs at each given moment, and there is our hope.

God is manifest everywhere and speaks through every

soul, not through self-appointed men dressed in costumes who pretend they know more than we do.

It is apparent everywhere that the Age of Aquarius has dawned. The age where Light shines on the earth exposing all the hypocrisy, so we can get rid of the darkness. Abusive religion will not survive.

When I left the Catholic Church, I did not lose my faith, I found the Truth. I have been protected and guided ever since. God does not abandon us!

Like the Great Oz, the curtain is being pulled away from the deceptive and powerful, exposing the little and vulnerable people hiding behind the throne.

I believe in miracles! I have been carried over fire and brimstone to this moment of healing and great joy. I give to you this story of myself to let you know there is no absolute law. There is simply God's unlimited, unconditional love.

THE END

Religious abuse is the misrepresentation of God with false beliefs that immobilize us with fear and guilt. We become victims of our own belief in our unworthiness and attract suffering to us. Listed below are some common abusive religious beliefs that limit our ability to experience the joy of spirituality, and positive beliefs centered in knowing we are divine souls that live in the Heart of God.

ABUSIVE RELIGIOUS BELIEFS	LIFE ENHANCING SPIRITUAL BELIEFS
1) Religion and God are the same.	Religion is man-made. God is Spirit.
2) Religion talks about God.	Spirituality experiences God.
3) I am a sinner.	I am Divine Spirit, offspring of God.
4) I am not worthy.	I am worthy, I am the Divine Child of God.
5) Suffering is the path to heaven.	Joy is the celebration of God. Heaven, the gift of joy.
6) We must constantly guard against evil.	We are always protected by spiritual guardians throughout life.

7) God judges us.

We judge ourselves.

8) God created suffering to punish us.

We are co-creators in free will. Our own fear has created suffering.

9) The Bible holds the only knowledge of God.

God cannot be contained in a book.

10) You must conform and obey religious leaders.

We must listen to our inner voice to know the Truth.

11) Women are spiritually inferior.

The soul has no gender and is equal in divinity.

12) Only appointed clergy know God.

All who desire know God.

13) God created eternal hell.

Religion created hell to keep us separate from Divine Unity.

14) Fear is necessary to control our evil nature.

Fear is the absence of Faith.